COTTAGE ECONOMY:

CONTAINING

Information relative to the brewing of BEER, making
of BREAD, keeping of COWS, PIGS, BEES, EWES, GOATS,
POULTRY and RABBITS, and relative to other matters
deemed useful in the conducting of the Affairs of a
Labourer's Family; to which are added, instructions
relative to the selecting, the cutting and the bleaching
of the Plants of ENGLISH GRASS and GRAIN, for the
purpose of making HATS and BONNETS.

BY WILLIAM COBBETT.

A NEW EDITION.

LONDON:

Printed for J. M. Cobbett, Fleet Street.

1823.

© in reprint 1974, 1976
LANDSMAN'S BOOKSHOP LTD.
BUCKENHILL, BROMYARD,
HEREFORDSHIRE, ENGLAND

ISBN 0 900513 06 3

Printed in Great Britain by R. B. Hall Ltd., Swadlincote

CONTENTS.

————

1 *2* *3*

COTTAGE ECONOMY.

No. I.

INTRODUCTION.

To the Labouring Classes of this Kingdom.

1. THROUGHOUT this little work, I shall *number* the Paragraphs, in order to be able, at some stages of the work, to refer, with the more facility, to parts that have gone before. The last Number will contain an *Index*, by the means of which the several matters may be turned to without loss of time; for, when *Economy* is the subject, *time* is a thing, which ought by no means to be overlooked.

2. The word *Economy*, like a great many others, has, in its application, been very much abused. It is generally used as if it meaned parsimony, stinginess, or niggardliness; and, at best, merely the refraining from expending money. Hence misers and close-fisted men disguise their propensity and conduct under the name of *Economy;* whereas the most liberal disposition, a disposition precisely the contrary of that of the miser, is perfectly consistent with economy.

3. ECONOMY means, *management*, and nothing more; and it is generally applied to the affairs of a house and family, which affairs are an object of

B

the greatest importance, whether as relating to individuals or to a nation. A nation is made powerful and to be honoured in the world not so much by the number of its people as by the ability and character of that people; and the ability and character of a people depend, in a great measure, upon the *economy* of the several families, which, all taken together, make up the nation. There never yet was, and never will be, a nation *permanently great*, consisting, for the greater part, of wretched and miserable families.

4. In every view of the matter, therefore, it is desirable, that the families of which a nation consists should be happily off; and, as this depends, in a great degree, upon the *management* of their concerns, the present work is intended to convey to the families of the *Labouring Classes* in particular, such information as I think may be useful with regard to that management.

5. I lay it down as a maxim, that, for a family to be happy, they must be well supplied with *food* and *raiment*. It is a sorry effort that people make to persuade others, or to persuade themselves, that they can be happy in a state of *want* of the necessaries of life. The doctrines, which fanaticism preaches, and which teach men to be *content* with *poverty*, have a very pernicious tendency, and are calculated to favour tyrants by giving them passive slaves. To live well, to enjoy all things that make life pleasant, is the right of every man who con-

stantly uses his strength judiciously and lawfully. It is to blaspheme God to suppose, that he created men to be miserable, to hunger, thirst, and perish with cold, in the midst of that abundance which is the fruit of their own labour. Instead, therefore, of applauding " *happy* poverty," which applause is so much the fashion of the present day, I despise the man that is *poor* and *contented ;* for, such content is a certain proof of a base disposition, a disposition which is the enemy of all industry, all exertion, all love of independence.

6. Let it be understood, however, that, by *poverty*, I mean *real want*, a real insufficiency of the food and raiment and lodging necessary to health and decency ; and not that imaginary poverty, of which some persons complain. The man, who, by his own and his family's labour, can provide a sufficiency of food and raiment and a comfortable dwelling place, is not a *poor man*. There must be different ranks and degrees in every civil society, and, indeed, so it is even amongst the savage tribes. There must be different degrees of wealth ; some must have more than others ; and the richest must be a great deal richer than the least rich. But, it is necessary to the very existence of a people, that nine out of ten should live wholly by the sweat of their brow ; and, is it not degrading to human nature, that all the nine tenths should be called *poor ;* and, what is still worse, *call themselves poor*, and be *contented* in that degraded state ?

B 2

7. The laws, the economy, or management, of a state may be such as to render it impossible for the labourer, however skilful and industrious, to maintain his family in health and decency; and, suc h has, for many years past, been the management of the affairs of this once truly great and happy land. A system of paper-money, the effect of which was to take from the labourer the half of his earnings, was what no industry and care could make head against. I do not pretend, that this system was adopted *by design.* But, no matter for the *cause;* such was the effect.

8. Better times, however, are approaching. The labourer now appears likely to obtain that hire of which he is worthy; and therefore, this appears to me to be the time to press upon him the *duty* of using his best exertions for the rearing of his family in a manner that must give him the best security for happiness to himself, his wife and children, and to make him, in all respects, what his forefathers were. The people of England have been famed, in all ages, for their *good living;* for the *abundance of their food* and *goodness of their attire.* The old sayings about English roast beef and plumb-pudding, and about English hospitality, had not their foundation in *nothing.* And, in spite of all the refinements of sickly minds, it is *abundant living* amongst the people at large, which is the great test of good government, and the surest basis of national greatness and security.

9. If the Labourer have his fair wages; if there be no false weights and measures, whether of money or of goods, by which he is defrauded; if the laws be equal in their effect on all men; if he be called upon for no more than his due share of the expenses necessary to support the government and defend the country, he has no reason to complain. If the largeness of his family demand extraordinary labour and care, these are due from him to it. He is the cause of the existence of that family; and, therefore, he is not, except in cases of accidental calamity, to throw upon others the burden of supporting it. Besides, " little children are as " arrows in the hands of the giant, and blessed is " the man that hath his quiver full of them." That is to say, children, if they bring their *cares*, bring also their *pleasures* and *solid advantages*. They become, very soon, so many assistants and props to the parents, who, when old age comes on, are amply repaid for all the toil and all the cares that children have occasioned in their infancy. To be without sure and safe friends in the world makes life not worth having; and whom can we be so sure of as of our children? Brothers and sisters are a mutual support. We see them, in almost every case, grow up into prosperity, when they act the part that the impulses of nature prescribe. When cordially united, a father and sons, or a family of brothers and sisters, may, in almost any state of life, set what is called misfortune at defiance.

10. These considerations are much more than enough to sweeten the toils and cares of parents, and to make them regard every additional child as an additional blessing. But, that children may be a blessing and not a curse, care must be taken of their *education.* This word has, of late years, been so perverted, so corrupted, so abused, in its application, that I am almost afraid to use it here. Yet I must not suffer it to be usurped by cant and tyranny. I must use it; but, not without clearly saying what I mean.

11. *Education* means *breeding up, bringing up,* or *rearing up;* and nothing more. This includes every thing with regard to the *mind* as well as the *body* of the child; but, of late years, it has been so used as to have no sense applied to it but that of *book-learning,* with which, nine times out of ten, it has nothing at all to do. It is, indeed, proper, and it is the duty of all parents, to teach, or cause to be taught, their children as much as they can of books, *after,* and not before, all the measures are safely taken for enabling them to get their living by labour, or, for *providing them a living without labour,* and that, too, out of the means obtained and secured by the parents out of their own income. The taste of the times is, unhappily, to give to children something of *book-learning,* with a view of placing them to live, in some way or other, *upon the labour of other people.* Very seldom, comparatively speaking, has this succeeded, even during the wasteful public expendi-

ture of the last thirty years; and, in the times that are approaching, it cannot, I thank God, succeed at all. When the project has failed, what disappointment, mortification and misery, to both parent and child! The latter is spoiled as a labourer; his book-learning has only made him conceited; into some course of desperation he falls; and the end is but too often not only wretched but ignominious.

12. Understand me clearly here, however; for, it is the duty of parents to give, if they be able, book-learning to their children, having *first* taken care to make them capable of earning their living by *bodily labour*. When that object has once been secured, the other may, if the ability remain, be attended to. But, I am wholly against children wasting their time in the idleness of what is called *education;* and particularly in schools over which the parents have no control, and where nothing is taught but the rudiments of servility, pauperism and slavery.

13. The *education* that I have in view is, therefore, of a very different kind. You should bear constantly in mind, that nine-tenths of us are, from the very nature and necessities of the world, born to gain our livelihood by the sweat of our brow. What reason have we, then, to presume, that our children are not to do the same? If they be, as now and then one will be, endued with extraordinary powers of mind, those powers may have an opportunity of developing themselves; and, if they never have that opportunity, the harm is not very great to us or to them.

Nor does it hence follow, that the descendants of labourers are *always* to be labourers. The path upwards is steep and long, to be sure. Industry, care,
skill, excellence in the present parent lays the foundation of *a rise,* under more favourable circumstances, for his children. The children of these take
another rise; and, by and by, the descendants of the
present labourer become gentlemen.

14. This is the natural progress. It is by attempt-
ing to reach the top at a *single leap* that so much
misery is produced in the world; and the propensity
to make such attempts has been cherished and en-
couraged by the strange projects that we have witnessed of late years for making the labourers *virtuous*
and *happy* by giving them what is called *education.*
The education which I speak of consists in bringing
children up to labour with *steadiness,* with *care,* and
with *skill;* to show them how to do as many useful
things as possible; to teach them to do them all in
the best manner; to set them an example in industry, sobriety, cleanliness and neatness; to make
all these *habitual* to them, so that they never shall
be liable to fall into the contrary; to let them always
see a *good living* proceeding from *labour,* and thus
to remove from them the temptation to get at the
goods of others by violent or fraudulent means, and
to keep far from their minds all the inducements to
hypocrisy and deceit.

15. And, bear in mind, that if the state of the labourer has its disadvantages when compared with

other callings and conditions of life, it has also its advantages. It is free from the torments of ambition, and from a great part of the causes of ill-health, for which not all the riches in the world and all the circumstances of high rank are a compensation. The able and prudent labourer is always *safe*, at the least; and that is what few men are who are lifted above him. They have losses and crosses to fear, the very thought of which never enters his mind, if he act well his part towards himself, his family and his neighbour.

16. But, the basis of good to him, is, *steady and skilful labour.* To assist him in the pursuit of this labour, and in the turning of it to the best account, are the principal objects of the present little work. I propose to treat of brewing Beer, making Bread, keeping Cows and Pigs, rearing Poultry, and of other matters; and to show, that, while, from a very small piece of ground, a large part of the food of a considerable family may be raised, the very act of raising it will be the best possible foundation of *education* of the children of the labourer; that it will teach them a great number of useful things, *add greatly to their value when they go forth from* their father's home, make them start in life with all possible advantages, and give them the best chance of leading happy lives. And, is it not much more rational for parents to be employed in teaching their children how to cultivate a garden, to feed and rear animals, to make bread, beer, bacon,

B 5

butter, and cheese, and to be able to do these things for themselves, or for others, than to leave them to prowl about the lanes and commons or to mope at the heels of some crafty, sleek-headed pretended saint, who while he extracts the last penny from their pockets, bids them be contented with their misery, and promises them, in exchange for their pence, everlasting glory in the world to come? It is upon the hungry and the wretched that the fanatic works. The dejected and forlorn are his prey. As an ailing carcass engenders vermin, a pauperized community engenders teachers of fanaticism, the very foundation of whose doctrines is, that we are to care nothing about this world, and that all our labours and exertions are in vain.

17. The man, who is doing well, who is in good health, who has a blooming and dutiful and cheerful and happy family about him, and who passes his day of rest amongst them, is not to be made to believe, that he was born to be miserable, and that poverty, the natural and just reward of laziness, is to secure him a crown of glory. Far be it from me to recommend a disregard of even outward observances as to matters of religion; but, can it be *religion*, to believe, that God has made us to be wretched and dejected? Can it be *religion* to regard, as marks of his grace, the poverty and misery that almost invariably attend our neglect to use the means of obtaining a competence in worldly things? Can it be *religion* to regard as blessings those things, those

very things, which God expressly numbers amongst his curses? Poverty never finds a place amongst the *blessings* promised by God. His blessings are of a directly opposite description; flocks, herds, corn, wine and oil; a smiling land; a rejoicing people; abundance for the body and gladness of the heart: these are the blessings which God promises to the industrious, the sober, the careful, and the upright. Let no man, then, believe, that, to be poor and wretched is a mark of God's favour; and let no man remain in that state, if he, by any honest means, can rescue himself from it.

18. Poverty leads to all sorts of evil consequences. *Want*, horrid want, is the great parent of crime. To have a dutiful family, the father's principle of rule must be *love* not *fear*. His sway must be gentle, or he will have only an unwilling and short-lived obedience. But, it is given to but few men to be gentle and good humoured amidst the various torments attendant on pinching poverty. A competence is, therefore, the first thing to be thought of; it is the foundation of all good in the labourer's dwelling; without it little but misery can be expected. " *Health,* " *peace,* and *competence,*" one of the wisest of men regards as the only things needful to man; but the two former are scarcely to be had without the latter. *Competence* is the foundation of happiness and of exertion. Beset with wants, having a mind continually harassed with fears of starvation, who can act with energy, who can calmly think? To

provide a *good living*, therefore, for himself and family, is the *very first duty* of every man. "Two things," says Agur, "have I asked; deny me them "not before I die: remove far from me vanity and "lies; give me neither poverty nor riches; feed me "with food convenient for me: lest I be full and "deny thee; or lest I be poor and steal."

19. A *good living*, therefore, a *competence*, is the first thing to be desired and to be sought after; and, if this little work should have the effect of aiding only a small portion of the Labouring Classes in securing that competence, it will afford great gratification to their friend,   Wm. COBBETT.

Kensington, 19 *July*, 1821.

BREWING BEER.

20. Before I proceed to give any directions about brewing, let me mention some of the inducements to do the thing. In former times, to set about to show to Englishmen that it was good for them to brew beer in their houses would have been as impertinent as gravely to insist, that they ought to endeavour not to lose their breath; for, in those times (only forty years ago), to have a *house* and not to brew was a rare thing indeed. Mr. Ellman, an old man and a large farmer, in Sussex, has recently given in Evidence, before a Committee of the House of Commons, this fact; that, *forty years ago*, there was

not a labourer in his parish that did not *brew his own beer;* and that *now,* there is *not one that does it,* except by chance the malt be given him. The causes of this change have been the lowering of the wages of labour, compared with the price of provisions, by the means of the paper-money, the enormous tax upon the barley when made into *malt,* and the increased tax upon *hops.* These have quite changed the customs of the English people as to their drink. They still drink *beer,* but, in general, it is of the brewing of *common brewers,* and in public houses, of which the common brewers have become the owners, and have thus, by the aid of paper-money, obtained a *monopoly* in the supplying of the great body of the people with one of those things, which to the hard-working man, is almost a necessary of life.

21. These things will be altered. They must be altered. The nation must be sunk into nothingness, or, a new system must be adopted ; and the nation will not sink into nothingness. The malt now pays a tax of 4*s.* 6*d.* a bushel, and the barley costs only 3*s.* This brings the bushel of malt to 8*s.* including the malster's charge for malting. If the tax were taken off the malt, malt would be sold, at the present price of barley, for about 3*s.* 3*d.* a bushel ; because a bushel of barley makes more than a bushel of malt, and the tax, besides its amount, causes great expenses of various sorts to the malster. The hops pay a tax of 2*d.* a pound ; and a

bushel of malt requires, in general, a pound of hops. If these two taxes were taken off, therefore, the consumption of barley and of hops would be exceedingly increased; for double the present quantity would be demanded, and the land is always ready to send it forth.

22. It appears impossible that the landlords should, much longer, submit to these intolerable burdens on their estates. In short, they must get off the malt tax, or lose those estates. They must do a great *deal more*, indeed; but that they must do at any rate. The paper-money is fast losing its destructive power; and things are, with regard to the labourers, coming back to what they were *forty years ago*, and, therefore, we may prepare for the making of beer in our own houses, and take leave of the poisonous stuff served out to us by common brewers. We may begin *immediately;* for, even at *present prices*, home-brewed beer is the *cheapest* drink that a family can use, except *milk*, and milk can be applicable only in certain cases.

23. The drink, which has come to supply the place of beer has, in general, been *tea*. It is notorious, that tea has no *useful strength* in it; that it contains nothing *nutricious;* that it, besides being *good* for nothing, has *badness* in it, because it is well known to produce want of sleep in many cases, and in all cases, to shake and weaken the nerves. It is, in fact, a weaker kind of laudanum, which enlivens for the moment and deadens afterwards. At any

rate it communicates no strength to the body; it does not, in any degree, assist in affording what labour demands. It is, then, of no *use*. And, now, as to its *cost*, compared with that of *beer*. I shall make my comparison applicable to a year, or three hundred and sixty-five days. I shall suppose the tea to be only five shillings the pound; the sugar only seven-pence; the milk only twopence a quart. The prices are at the very lowest. I shall suppose a tea-pot to cost a shilling, six cups and saucers two shillings and sixpence, and six pewter spoons eighteen pence. How to estimate the firing I hardly know; but certainly there must, in the course of the year, be two hundred fires made that would not be made, were it not for tea drinking. Then comes the great article of all, the *time* employed in this tea making affair. It is impossible to make a fire, boil water, make the tea, drink it, wash up the things, sweep up the fire-place and put all to rights again in a less space of time, upon an average, than *two hours*. However, let us allow *one hour;* and here we have a woman occupied no less than three hundred and sixty-five hours in the year, or, thirty whole days, at twelve hours in the day; that is to say, one month out of the twelve in the year, besides the waste of the man's time in hanging about waiting for the tea! Needs there any thing more to make us cease to wonder at seeing labourers' children with dirty linen and holes in the heels of their stockings? Observe, too, that the time thus spent, is, one half of it, the best time of the day. It is the top of the morning, which, in every calling of life, contains an hour worth two or three hours of the afternoon. By the time that the clattering tea tackle is out of the way, the morning is spoiled; its prime is gone; and any work that is to be done afterwards lags heavily along. If the mother have to go out to work, the tea affair must all first be over. She comes into the field, in Summer time, when the sun has gone a third part of his course. She has the heat of the day to encounter, instead of having her work done and being ready to return home at an early hour. Yet early she must go, too; for, there is the fire again to be made, the clattering tea tackle again to come forward; and even in the longest day she must have *candle light*, which never ought to be seen in a cottage (except in case of illness) from March to September.

24. Now, then, let us take the bare cost of the use of tea. I suppose a pound of tea to last twenty days; which is not nearly half an ounce every morning and evening. I allow for each mess half a pint of milk. And I allow three pounds of the red dirty sugar to each pound of tea. The account of expenditure would then stand very high; but to these must be added the amount of the tea tackle, one set of which will, upon an average, be demolished every year. To these outgoings must be added the cost of beer at the public house; for, some the man will have after all, and the woman too, unless they be upon

the point of actual starvation. Two pots a week is
as little as will serve in this way ; and here is a
dead loss of ninepence a week, seeing that two pots
of beer, full as strong, and a great deal better, can
be brewed at home for threepence. The account of
the year's tea drinking will, then, stand thus:

18lb. of Tea	-	-	-	£4	10	0
54lb. of Sugar	-	-	-	1	11	6
365 Pints of Milk	-	-	-	1	10	0
Tea Tackle	-	-	-	0	5	0
200 Fires	-	-	-	0	16	8
30 Day's works	-	-	-	0	15	0
Loss by going to public house				1	19	0
				£11	7	2

25.   I have here estimated every thing at its very
lowest.   The entertainment which I have here provided is as poor, as mean, as miserable as any thing
short of starvation can set forth ; and yet the wretched
thing amounts to a good third part of a good and able
labourer's wagers.   For this money, he and his
family may drink good and wholesome beer, and, in
a short time, out of the mere savings from this waste,
may drink it out of silver cups and tankards.   In a
labourer's family, *wholesome* beer, that has a little
life in it, is all that is wanted in *general.*   Little
children, that do not work, should not have beer.
Broth, porridge, or something in that way is the
thing for them.   However, I shall suppose, in order
to make my comparison as little complicated as possible, that he brews nothing but beer as strong as the
generality of beer to be had at the public house, and
divested of the poisonous drugs which that beer but

too often contains; and I shall further suppose that he uses in his family two quarts of this beer every day from the first of October to the last day of March inclusive; three quarts a day during the months of April and May; four quarts a day during the months of June and September; and five quarts a day during the months of July and August; and if this be not enough it must be a family of drunkards. Here are 1097 quarts, or, 274 gallons. Now, a bushel of malt will make eighteen gallons of better beer than that which is sold at the public houses. And this is precisely a gallon for the price of a quart. People should bear in mind, that the beer, bought at the public house, is loaded with a *beer tax*, with the tax on the public house keeper, in the shape of licence, with all the taxes and expenses of the brewer, with all the taxes, rent and other expenses of the publican, and with all the *profits* of both brewer and publican; so that when a man swallows a pot of beer at a public house, he has all these expenses to help to defray, besides the mere tax on the malt and on the hops,

26. Well, then, to brew this ample supply of good beer for a labourer's family; these 274 gallons, requires *fifteen* bushels of malt and (for let us do the thing well) *fifteen pounds of hops*. The malt is now eight shillings a bushel, and very good hops may be bought for less than a shilling a pound. The *grains* and *yeast* will amply pay for the labour and fuel employed in the brewing; seeing that there will be pigs

to eat the grains, and bread to be baked with the
yeast. The account will, then, stand thus:

	£	s.	d.
15 bushels of Malt - - -	6	0	0
15 pounds of Hops - - -	0	15	0
Wear of Utensils - - -	0	10	0
	£7	5	0

27. Here, then, is the sum of four pounds, two shillings and twopence saved every year. The utensils for
brewing are, a brass kettle, a mashing tub, coolers (for
which washing tubs may serve), a half hogshead,
with one end taken out for a tun tub, about four nine
gallon casks, and a couple of eighteen gallon casks.
This is an ample supply of utensils, each of which
will last with proper care a good long lifetime or
two, and the whole of which, even if purchased new
from the shop, will only exceed by a few shillings, if
they exceed at all, the amount of the saving, arising
the very first year, from quitting the troublesome and
pernicious practice of drinking tea. The saving of
each succeeding year would, if you chose it, purchase
a silver mug to hold half a pint at least. However,
the saving would naturally be applied to purposes
more conducive to the well-being and happiness of a
family.

28. It is not, however, the *mere saving* to which I
look. This is, indeed, a matter of great importance,
whether we look at the amount itself, or at the ultimate consequences of a judicious application of it;
for, *four pounds* make a great *hole* in a man's wages
for the year; and when we consider all the advan-

tages that would arise to a family of children from having these four pounds, now so miserably wasted, laid out upon their backs, in the shape of decent dress, it is impossible to look at this waste without feelings of sorrow not wholly unmixed with those of a harsher description.

29. But, I look upon the thing in a still more serious light. I view the tea drinking as a destroyer of health, an enfeebler of the frame, an engenderer of effeminacy and laziness, a debaucher of youth, and a maker of misery for old age. In the fifteen bushels of malt, there are 570 pounds weight of *sweet;* that is to say of nutricious matter, unmixed with any thing injurious to health. In the 730 tea messes of the year there are 54 pounds of sweet in the sugar and about thirty pounds of matter equal to sugar in the milk. Here are eighty-four pounds, instead of five hundred and seventy, and even the good effect of these eighty-four pounds is more than overbalanced by the corrosive, gnawing, the poisonous powers of the tea.

30. It is impossible for any one to deny the truth of this statement. Put it to the test with a lean hog: give him the fifteen bushels of malt, and he will repay you in ten score of bacon or thereabouts. But give him the 730 tea messes, or rather begin to give them to him, and give him nothing else, and he is dead with hunger, and bequeaths you his skeleton, at the end of about seven days. It is impossible to doubt in such a case. The tea drinking has done a

great deal in bringing this nation into the state fo misery in which it now is; and the tea drinking, which is carried on by "dribs" and "drabs;" by pence and farthings going out at a time; this miserable practice has been gradually introduced by the growing weight of the taxes on Malt and on Hops, and by the everlasting penury amongst the labourers, occasioned by the paper-money.

31. We see better prospects, however, and therefore let us now rouse ourselves, and shake from us the degrading curse, the effects of which have been much more extensive and infinitely more mischievous than men in general seem to imagine.

32. It must be evident to every one, that the practice of tea drinking must render the frame feeble and unfit to encounter hard labour or severe weather, while, as I have shown, it deducts from the means of replenishing the belly and covering the back. Hence succeeds a softness, an effeminacy, a seeking for the fire side, a lurking in the bed, and, in short, all the characteristics of idleness, for which, in this case, real want of strength furnishes an apology. The tea drinking fills the public house, makes the frequenting of it habitual, corrupts boys as soon as they are able to move from home, and does little less for the girls, to whom the gossip of the tea table is no bad preparatory school for the brothel. At the very least, it teaches them idleness. The everlasting dawdling about with the slops of the tea tackle gives them a relish for nothing that re-

quires strength and activity. When they go from home, they know how to do nothing that is useful. To brew, to bake, to make butter, to milk, to rear poultry; to do any earthly thing of use they are wholly unqualified. To shut poor young creatures up in Manufactories is bad enough; but there at any rate, they do something that is useful; whereas the girl that has been brought up merely to boil the tea kettle, and to assist in the gossip inseparable from the practice, is a mere consumer of food, a pest to her employer, and a curse to her husband, if any man be so unfortunate as to fix his affections upon her.

33. But, is it in the power of any man, any good labourer who has attained the age of fifty, to look back upon the last thirty years of his life, without cursing the day in which tea was introduced into England? Where is there such a man, who cannot trace to this cause, a very considerable part of all the mortifications and sufferings of his life? When was he ever *too late* at his labour; when did he ever meet with a frown, with a turning off and pauperism on that account, without being able to trace it to the tea kettle? When reproached with lagging in the morning, the poor wretch tells you, that he will make up for it by *working during his breakfast time!* I have heard this a hundred and a hundred times over. He was up time enough; but the tea kettle kept him lolling and lounging at home; and now instead of sitting down to a breakfast upon bread, bacon and

beer, which is to carry him on to the hour of dinner, he has to force his limbs along under the sweat of feebleness, and at dinner time to swallow his dry bread, or sleak his half feverish thirst at the pump or the brook. To the wretched tea kettle he has to return at night with legs hardly sufficient to maintain him; and thus he makes his miserable progress towards that death which he finds ten or fifteen years sooner than he would have found it had he made his wife brew beer instead of making tea. If he now and then gladden his heart with the drugs of the public house, some quarrel, some accident, some illness is the probable consequence; to the affray abroad succeeds an affray at home; the mischievous example reaches the children, corrupts them or scatters them, and misery for life is the consequence.

34. I should now proceed to the *details* of Brewing; but these, though they will not occupy a large space, must be put off to the *second Number*. The custom of brewing at home has so long ceased, amongst labourers, and, in many cases, amongst tradesmen, that it was necessary for me fully to state my reasons for wishing to see the custom revived. I shall, in my next, clearly explain how the operation is performed; and, it will be found to be so *easy a thing*, that I am not without hope, that many *tradesmen*, who now spend their evenings at the public house amidst tobacco smoke and empty noise, may be induced, by the finding of better drink at home at a quarter part of the price, to perceive that home

is by far the pleasantest place wherein to pass their hours of relaxation.

35. My work is intended chiefly for the benefit of *cottagers*, who must, of course, have some *land;* for, I propose to show, that a large part of the food of even a large family may be raised, without any diminution of the labourer's earnings abroad, from 40 rod, or a quarter of an acre, of ground; but at the same time, what I have to say will be applicable to larger establishments, in all the branches of domestic economy; and especially to that of providing a family with *beer.*

36. The *kind of beer* for a labourer's family; that is to say, the *degree of strength*, must depend on circumstances; on the numerousness of the family, on the season of the year, and various other. But, generally speaking, beer *half* the strength of that mentioned in Paragraph 25 will be quite strong enough; for that is, at least, one-third stronger than the farm-house " *small beer*," which, however, as long experience has proved, is best suited to the purpose. A judicious labourer would, probably, always have some *ale* in his house, and have small beer for the general drink. There is no reason why he should not keep *Christmas* as well as the farmer; and when he is *mowing*, *reaping*, or is at any other hard work, a quart, or three pints of *really good fat ale* a-day is by no means too much. However, circumstances vary so much with different labourers, that, as to the *sort* of beer and the number of brew-

ings and the times of brewing no general rule can be laid d ow

37. Before I proceed to explain the uses of the several brewing utensils, I must speak of the *quality* of the materials of which beer is made ; that is to say, the *malt*, *hops*, and *water*. Malt varies very much in quality, as, indeed, it must, with the quality of the barley. When good it is full of flour, and in biting a grain asunder, you find it bite easily, and see the *shell thin* and filled up well with flour. If it bite *hard* and *steely*, the malt is bad. There is *pale* malt and *brown* malt ; but the difference in the two arises merely from the different degrees of heat employed in the drying. The main thing to attend to, is, the *quantity of flour*. If the barley was bad ; *thin*, or *steely*, whether from unripeness or blight, or any other cause, it will not *malt* so well ; that is to say, it will not send out its roots in due time ; and a part of it will still be barley. Then, the world is wicked enough to think, and even to say, that there are maltsters, who, when they send you a bushel of malt, *put a little barley amongst it*, the malt being *taxed* and the barley *not!* Let us hope, that this is seldom the case ; yet, when we *do know* that this terrible system of taxation induces the beer-selling gentry to supply their customers with stuff little better than poison, it is not very uncharitable to suppose it possible for some maltsters to yield to the temptations of the Devil so far as to play the trick above mentioned. To detect this trick, and to dis-

c

cover what portion of the barley is in an unmalted state, take a handful of the *unground* malt, and put it into a bowl of cold water. Mix it about with the water a little; that is, let every grain be *just wet all over*; and whatever part of them *sink* are not *good*. If you have your malt *ground*, there is not, that I know of, any means of detection. Therefore, if your brewing be considerable in amount, *grind your own malt*, the means of doing which is very easy, and neither expensive nor troublesome, as will appear, when I come to speak of *flour*. If the barley be all *well malted*, there is still a variety in the quality of the malt; that is to say, a bushel of malt from fine, plump, heavy barley, will be better than the same quantity from thin and light barley. In this case, as in the case of wheat, the *weight* is the criterion of the quality. Only, bear in mind, that as a bushel of wheat, weighing *sixty-two* pounds, is better worth *six* shillings, than a bushel, weighing *fifty-two* is worth *four* shillings, so a bushel of malt weighing *forty-five* pounds is better worth *nine* shillings, than a bushel, weighing *thirty-five* is worth *six* shillings. In malt, therefore, as in every thing else, the word *cheap* is a deception, unless the quality be taken into view. But, bear in mind, that, in the case of *unmalted* barley mixed with the malt, the *weight* can be no rule; for barley is *heavier* than malt.

BREWING BEER.

(continued.)

38. AS to using *barley* in the making of beer, I have given it a full and fair trial twice over; and, I would recommend it to neither rich nor poor. The barley produces *strength*, though nothing like the malt; but, the beer is *flat*, even though you use half malt and half barley; and, flat beer lies heavy on the stomach, and, of course, besides the bad taste, is unwholesome. To pay 4*s*. 6*d*. tax upon every bushel of our own barley turned into malt, when the barley itself is not worth 3*s*. a bushel, is a horrid thing; but, as long as the owners of the land shall be so dastardly as to suffer themselves to be thus deprived of the use of their estates to favour the slave-drivers and plunderers of the East and West Indies, we must submit to the thing, incomprehensible to foreigners, and even to ourselves, as the submission may be.

39. With regard to *Hops*, the quality is very various. At times when some sell for 5*s*. a pound, others sell for *sixpence*. Provided the purchaser understand the article, the quality is, of course, in proportion to the price. There are two things to be considered in hops: the *power of preserving beer*, and that of giving it a *pleasant flavour*.

c 2

Hops may be *strong*, and yet not *good*. They should be *bright*, have no *leaves* or bits of branches amongst them. The hop is the *husk*, or *seed-pod*, of the hop-vine, as the *cone* is that of the fir-tree; and the *seeds* themselves are deposited, like those of the fir, round a little soft stalk, enveloped by the several folds of this pod, or cone. If, in the gathering, leaves of the vine or bits of the branches, are mixed with the hops, these not only help to make up the *weight*, but they give a *bad taste* to the beer; and, indeed, if they abound much, they spoil the beer. Great attention is, therefore, necessary in this respect. There are, too, numerous *sorts* of hops, varying in size, form, and quality, quite as much as *apples*. However, when they are in a state to be used in brewing, the marks of goodness are, an absence of *brown colour* (for that indicates *perished* hops); a colour *between green and yellow;* a great *quantity of the yellow farina;* seeds *not too large nor too hard;* a *clammy feel* when rubbed between the fingers; and a *lively* pleasant smell. As to the *age* of hops, they retain for twenty years, probably, their *power of preserving beer ;* but not of giving it a pleasant flavour. I have used them at *ten years old*, and should have no fear of using them at twenty. They lose none of their *bitterness;* none of their power of preserving beer; but, they lose the other quality; and, therefore, in the making of fine ale or beer, new hops are to be preferred. As to the *quantity* of hops, it is clear, from what has been said, that that must, in some degree depend upon their *quality ;* but, supposing them to be good in quality, a pound of hops to a bushel of malt is aout the quantity. A good deal, however, depends upon the length of time that the beer is intended to be kept, and upon the season of the year in which it is brewed. Beer intended to be kept a long while should have the full pound, also beer brewed in warmer weather, though, for present use, half the quantity may do under an opposite state of circum-stances.

40. The *Water* should be *soft* by all means. That of brooks, or rivers, is best. That of a *pond*, fed by a rivulet, or spring, will do very well. *Rain-water*, if just fallen, may do ; but stale rain-water, or stag-nant pond-water, makes the beer *flat* and difficult to keep ; and *hard* water, from wells, is very bad : it does not get the sweetness out of the malt nor the bitterness out of the hops, like soft water ; and the wort of it does not ferment well, which is a certain proof of its unfitness for the purpose.

41. There are two descriptions of persons whom I am desirous to see brewing their own beer ; name-ly, *tradesmen*, and *labourers* and *journeymen*. There must, therefore, be two *distinct scales* treated of. In the former editions of this work, I spoke of a *Machine* for brewing, and stated the advantages of using it in a family of any considerable consumption of beer, but, while, from my desire to promote *private brew-ing*, I strongly recommended the *machine*, I stated;

that, " if any of my readers could point out any " method, by which we should be more likely to re- " store the practice of private brewing, and espe- " cially to the *Cottage*, I should be greatly obliged " to them to communicate it to me." Such commu- nications have been made, and I am very happy to be able, in this new edition of my little work, to avail myself of them. There was, in the *Patent Machine*, always an objection on account of the *ex- pense;* for, even the machine for *one bushel of malt* cost, at the reduced price, *eight pounds,* a sum far above the reach of *a cottager,* and even above that of a small tradesman. Its *convenience*, especially in *towns*, where room is so valuable, was an object of great importance; but, there were *disadvantages* attending it, which, until after some experience, I did not ascertain. It will be remembered, that the method by the Brewing Machine requires the malt to be put into *the cold water*, and for the water to make the malt *swim*, or, at least, to be in such pro- portion as to prevent the fire beneath from burning the malt. We found, that our beer was *flat*, and that it did *not keep*. And this arose, I have every reason to believe, from this process. The malt should be *put into hot water*, and the water, at first, should be but just sufficient in quantity to *stir the malt in*, and *separate it well*. Nevertheless, when it is merely to make *small beer;* beer *not wanted to keep;* in such cases the Brewing Machine may be of use; and, as will be seen by-and-by, a moveable *boiler* (which has nothing to do with the *patent)* may, in many cases, be of great convenience and utility.

42. The two *scales*, of which I have spoken above, are now to be spoken of; and, that I may explain my meaning the more clearly, I shall suppose, that, for the tradesman's family, it will be requisite to brew eighteen gallons of ale and thirty-six of small beer, to fill three casks of eighteen gallons each. It will be observed, of course, that, for larger quantities, larger utensils of all sorts will be wanted. I take this quantity as the one to give directions on. The utensils wanted here will be, First, A *copper* that will contain *forty gallons* at least; for, though there be to be but thirty-six gallons of small beer, there must be space for the hops, and for the liquor that goes off in steam. Second, A *mashing-tub* to contain sixty gallons; for the malt is to be in this along with the water. Third, An *underbuck*, or shallow tub to go under the mash-tub for the wort to run into when drawn from the grains. Fourth, A *tun-tub*, that will contain thirty gallons, to put the ale into to work, the mash-tub, as we shall see, serving as a tun-tub for the small beer. Besides these, a couple of *coolers*, shallow tubs, which may be the heads of wine butts, or some such things, about a foot deep; or, if you have *four* it may be as well, in order to effect the cooling more quickly.

43. You begin by filling the copper with water, and next by making the water *boil*. You then put

into the mashing-tub water sufficient *to stir and separate the malt in*. But, now let me say more particularly what this mashing-tub is· It is, you know, to contain *sixty gallons*. It is to be a little broader at top than at bottom, and not quite so deep as it is wide across the bottom. In the middle of the bottom there is a hole about two inches over, to draw the wort off through. Into this hole goes a stick a foot or two longer than the tub is high. This stick is to be about two inches through, and *tapered* for about eight inches upwards at the end that goes into the hole, which at last it fills up closely as a cork. Upon the hole, before any thing else be put into the tub, you lay a little bundle of *fine birch* (heath or straw *may* do) about half the bulk of a birch broom, and well tied at both ends. This being laid over the hole (to keep back the grains as the wort goes out) you put the tapered end of the stick down through into the hole, and thus *cork* the hole up. You must then have something of weight sufficient to keep the birch steady at the bottom of the tub, with a hole through it to slip down the stick; otherwise when the stick is raised it will be apt to raise the birch with it, and when you are stirring the mash you would move it from its place. The best thing for this purpose will be a *leaden collar* for the stick, with the hole in the collar plenty large enough, and it should weigh three or four pounds. The thing they use in some farm-houses is the iron box of a wheel. Any thing will do that will slide down the stick, and lie with weight enough on the birch to keep it from moving. Now, then, you are ready to begin brewing. I allow *two bushels* of malt for the brewing I have supposed. You must now put into the mashing-tub as much boiling water as will be sufficient to *stir the malt in* and *separate it well.* But, here occurs one of the nicest points of all: namely, the *degree of heat* that the water is to be at, before you put in the malt. This heat is *one hundred and seventy degrees* by the thermometer. If you have a thermometer, this is ascertained easily; but, without one, take this rule, by which so much good beer has been made in England for hundreds of years: when you can, by looking down into the tub, *see your face clearly in the water.* the water is become cool enough; and you must not put the malt in before. Now put in the malt and *stir it well in the water.* To perform this stirring, which is very necessary, you have a stick, somewhat bigger than a broom-stick, with two or three smaller sticks, eight or ten inches long, put through the lower end of it at about three or four inches asunder, and sticking out on each side of the long stick. These small cross sticks serve to search the malt and separate it well in the stirring or *mashing.* Thus, then, the *malt is in;* and, in this state it should continue for about a quarter of an hour. In the meanwhile you will have filled up your copper, and made it *boil;* and now (at the end of the quarter of an hour) you put in boiling water sufficient to give you your

c 5

eighteen gallons of *ale*. But, perhaps, you must have thirty gallons of water in the whole; for, the grains will retain at least ten gallons of water; and it is better to have rather too much wort than too little. When your proper quantity of water is in, stir the malt again well. Cover the mashing-tub over with *sacks*, or something that will answer the same purpose; and there let the mash stand for *two hours*. When it has stood the two hours, you draw off the wort. And now, mind, the mashing-tub is placed on a *couple of stools*, or on something, that will enable you to put the *underbuck* under it, so as to receive the wort as it comes out of the hole before mentioned. When you have put the underbuck in its place, you let out the wort by pulling up the stick that corks the hole. But, observe, this stick (which goes six or eight inches through the hole,) must be raised by degrees, and the wort must be let out *slowly*, in order to keep back the *sediment*. So that, it is necessary to have something to *keep the stick up* at the point where you are to raise it, and wish to fix it at for the time. To do this, the simplest, cheapest and best thing in the world is a *cleft stick*. Take a *rod* of ash, hazle, birch, or almost any wood; let it be a foot or two longer than your mashing-tub is wide over the top; *split* it, as if for making hoops; tie it round with a string at each end; lay it across your mashing-tub; pull it open in the middle and let the upper part of the wort-stick through it; and, when you raise that stick, by degrees as before directed, the cleft stick *will hold it up* at whatever height you please.

44. When you have drawn off the *ale-wort*, you proceed to put into the mashing-tub water for the *small beer*. But, I shall go on with my directions about the *Ale*, till I have got into the *cask* and *cellar;* and shall then return to the small-beer.

45. As you draw off the ale-wort into the under-buck, you must lade it out of that into the tun-tub, for which work, as well as for various other purposes in the brewing, you must have a *bowl-dish* with a handle to it. The underbuck will not hold the whole of the wort. It is, as before described, a shallow tub, to go *under* the mashing-tub to draw off the wort into. Out of this underbuck you must lade the ale-wort into the *tun-tub;* and there it must remain till your *copper* be emptied and ready to receive it.

46. The copper being empty, you put the wort into it, and put in after the wort, or before it, *a pound and a half of good hops*, well rubbed and separated as you put them in. You now make the copper boil, and keep it, with the lid off, at a good *brisk* boil for a *full hour,* and if it be an hour and a half, it is none the worse.

47. When the boiling is done, put out your fire, and put the liquor into the *coolers.* But it must be put into the coolers *without the hops.* Therefore, in order to get the hops out of the liquor, you must have a *strainer.* The best for your purpose is a small *clothes-basket*, or any other wicker-basket. You set

your coolers in the most convenient place. It may
be in-doors or out of doors, as most convenient. You
lay a couple of sticks across one of the coolers, and
put the basket upon them. Put your liquor, hops
and all, into the basket, which will *keep back the
hops*. When you have got enough liquor in one
cooler, you go to another with your sticks and basket,
till you have got all your liquor out. If you find
your liquor deeper in one cooler than the other, you
can make an alteration in that respect, till you have
the liquor so distributed as to cool equally fast in
both, or all, the coolers.

48. The next stage of the liquor is in the *tun-tub*,
where it is *set to work*. Now, a very great point is,
the *degree of heat* that the liquor is to be at, when it is
set to working. The proper heat is seventy degrees ;
so that a thermometer makes this matter sure. In the
country they determine the degree of heat by merely
putting a finger into the liquor. Seventy degrees is
but *just warm*, a gentle *luke-warmth*. Nothing like
heat. A little experience makes perfectness in such
a matter. When at the proper heat, or nearly (for
the liquor will cool a little in being removed), put it
into the *tun-tub*. And, now, before I speak of the
act of setting the beer to work, I must describe this
tun-tub, which I first mentioned in Paragraph 42.
It is to hold *thirty gallons*, as you have seen ; and
nothing is better than an old *cask* of that size, or
somewhat larger, with the head taken out, or cut off.
But, indeed, any tub of sufficient dimensions, and of

about the same depth proportioned to the width, as a cask or barrel has, will do for the purpose. Having put the liquor into the tun-tub, you put in *the yeast*. About *half a pint* of good yeast is sufficient. This should first be put into a thing of some sort that will hold about a gallon of your liquor; the thing should then be nearly filled with liquor and with a stick or spoon, you should mix the yeast well with the liquor in this bowl, or other thing, and stir in along with the yeast, a handful of *wheat or rye flour*. This mixture is then to be poured out clean into the tun-tub, and the whole mass of the liquor is then to be agitated well, by lading up and pouring down again with your bowl-dish, till the yeast be well mixed with the liquor. Some people do the thing in another manner. They mix up the yeast and flour with some liquor (as just mentioned) taken out of the coolers; and then they set the little vessel that contains this mixture down *on the bottom of the tun-tub;* and, leaving it there, put the liquor out of the coolers into the tun-tub. Being placed at the bottom, and having the liquor poured on it, the mixture is, perhaps, more perfectly effected in this way than in any way. The *flour* may not be necessary ; but, as the country-people use it, it is, doubtless, of some use ; for, their hereditary experience has not been for nothing. When your liquor is thus properly put into the tun-tub and set a working, cover over the top of the tub by laying across it a sack or two, or something that will answer the purpose.

49. We now come to the *last stage;* the *cask* or *barrel.* But I must first speak of the place for the tun-tub to stand in. The place should be such as to avoid too much warmth or cold. The air should, if possible, be at about 55 degrees. Any cool place in summer, and any *warmish* place in winter. If the weather be *very cold,* some cloths or sacks should be put round the tun-tub while the beer is working. In about six or eight hours a *frothy* head will rise upon the liquor; and it will keep rising, more or less slowly, for about forty-eight hours. But, the *length of time* required for the working depends on various circumstances; so that no precise time can be fixed. The best way is, to take off the froth (which is indeed *yeast*) at the end of about twenty-four hours, with a common skimmer, and put it into a pan or vessel of some sort; then, in twelve hours' time, take it off again in the same way; and so on till the liquor has *done working,* and sends up no more yeast. Then it is *beer;* and, when it is *quite cold* (for *ale* or *strong beer*) put it into the *cask* by means of a *funnel.* It must be cold before you do this; or, it will be what the country-people call *foxed;* that is to say, have a rank and disagreeable taste. Now, as to the *cask,* it must be *sound* and *sweet.* I thought, when writing the former edition of this work, that the *bell-shaped* were the best casks. I am now convinced that that was an error. The bell-shaped, by contracting the width of the top of the beer, as that top descends in consequence of the draft for use, certainly prevents the *head* (which always gathers on beer as soon as you begin to draw it off) from breaking and mixing in amongst the beer. This is an advantage in the bell-shape; but, then, the bell-shape, which places the widest end of the cask uppermost, exposes the cask to the admission of *external air* much more than the other shape. This danger approaches from the *ends* of the cask; and, in the bell-shape, you have the *broadest* end wholly exposed the moment you have drawn out the first gallon of beer, which is not the case with the casks of the common shape. Directions are given, in the case of the bell-casks, to put *damp sand* on the top to keep out the air. But, it is very difficult to make this effectual; and, yet, if you do not keep out the air, your beer will be *flat;* and, when flat, it really is good for nothing but the pigs. It is very difficult to *fill* the bell cask, which you will easily see if you consider its shape. It must be placed on the *level* with the greatest possible *truth*, or there will be a space left; and, to place it with such truth is, perhaps, as difficult a thing as mason, or bricklayer, ever has to perform. And yet, if this be not done, there will be an *empty space* in the cask, though it may, at the same time, run over. With the common casks, there are none of these difficulties. A common eye will see when it is well placed; and, at any rate, any little vacant space that may be left is not at an *end* of the cask, and will, without great carelessness, be so small as to be of no consequence. We now come to the act of putting in the beer. The cask should be placed on a stand with legs about a foot long. The cask, being round, must have a little wedge, or block, on each side to keep it steady. *Bricks* do very well. Bring your beer down into the cellar in buckets, and pour it in through the funnel, until the cask be full. The cask should *lean a little on one side* when you fill it; because the beer will *work again* here, and send more yeast out of the bung-hole; and, if the cask were not a little on one side, the yeast would flow over both sides of the cask, and would not descend in *one stream* into a pan, put underneath to receive it. Here the bell-cask is extremely inconvenient; for the yeast works up all *over the head*, and *cannot run off*, and makes a very nasty affair. This *alone*, to say nothing of the other disadvantages, would decide the question against the bell-casks. Something will *go off in this working*, which may continue for two or three days. When you put the beer in the cask, you should have a *gallon or two left*, to keep filling up with as the working produces emptiness. At last, when the working is completely over, *right* the cask. That is to say, block it up to its level. Put in a handful of *fresh hops*. Fill the cask quite full. Put in the bung, with a bit of *coarse linen* stuff round it; hammer it down tight; and, if you like, fill a coarse bag with sand, and lay it, well pressed down, over the bung.

50. As to the length of time that you are to keep the beer before you begin to use it, that must, in some measure, depend on taste. *Such beer* as this *ale*, will keep almost any length of time. As to the mode of *tapping*, that is as easy almost as *drinking*. When the cask is *empty*, great care must be taken to cork it *tightly up*, so that no air get in; for, if it do, the cask is *moulded*, and when once moulded it is *spoiled for ever*. It is never again fit to be used about beer. Before the cask be used again, the grounds must be poured out, and the cask cleaned by several times scalding; by putting in *stones* (or a *chain*), and rolling and shaking about, till it be quite clean. Here again the round casks have the decided advantage; it being almost impossible to make the bell-casks thoroughly clean without *taking the head out*, which is both troublesome and expensive; as it cannot be well done by any one but a *cooper*, who is not always at hand, and who, when he is, must be *paid*.

51. I have now done with the *ale*, and it remains for me to speak of the *small beer*. In Paragraph 47 (which now see) I left you drawing off the *ale-wort*, and with your copper full of boiling water. Thirty-six gallons of that boiling water are, as soon as you have got your ale-wort out, and have put down your mash-tub stick to close up the hole at the bottom; as soon as you have done this, 36 gallons of the boiling-water are to go into the mashing-tub; the grains are to be well stirred up, as before;

the mashing-tub is to be covered over again, as mentioned in Paragraph 43 ; and the mash is to stand in that state for *an hour*; and not two hours, as for the ale-wort.

52. When the small beer mash has stood its hour, draw it off as in Paragraph 47, and put it into the tun-tub, as you did the ale-wort.

53. By this time your copper will be *empty* again, by putting your ale-liquor to cool, as mentioned in Paragraph 47. And you now put the small beer wort *into the copper* with the hops that you used before, and with *half a pound of fresh hops* added to them ; and this liquor you boil briskly for *an hour.*

54. By this time you will have taken the grains and the sediment clean out of the mashing-tub, and taken out the bunch of birch twigs, and made all clean. Now put in the birch twigs again, and put down your stick as before. Lay your two or three sticks across the mashing-tub, put your basket or them, and take your liquor from the copper (putting the fire out first) and pour it into the mashing-tub through the basket. Take the basket away, throw the hops to the dunghill, and leave the small beer liquor *to cool in the mashing-tub.*

55. Here it is to remain to be *set to working* as mentioned for the ale in Paragraph 48 ; only, in this case, you will want *more yeast in proportion;* and should have for your 36 gallons of small beer, three half pints of good yeast.

56. Proceed, as to all the rest of the business, as with the ale, only, in the case of the small beer, it should be put into the cask, not *quite cold;* but a *little warm ;* or else it will not work at all in the barrel, which it ought to do. It will not work so strongly nor so long as the ale ; and may be put in the barrel much sooner: in general the next day after it is brewed.

57. All the utensils should be well cleaned and put away as soon as they are done with ; the *little* things as well as the great things ; for it is *loss of time* to make new ones. And, now, let us see the *expense* of these utensils. The copper, *new,* 5*l.* the mashing-tub, *new,* 30*s.* the tun-tub, not new, 5*s.* the underbuck and three coolers, not new, 20*s.* The whole cost is, 7*l.* 10*s.* which is ten shillings less than the *one bushel Machine.* I am now in a farm-house, where the *same set* of utensils has been used for *forty years;* and the owner tells me, that, with the same use, they may last for *forty years longer.* The Machine will not, I think, last *four years*, if in any thing like regular use. It is of sheet-iron, *tinned on the inside,* and this tin *rusts* exceedingly, and is not to be kept clean without such *rubbing* as must soon take off the tin. The great advantage of the Machine is, that it can be *removed.* You can brew without a *brew-house.—* You can set the boiler up against any fire-place, or any window. You can brew under a cart-shed, or, even out of doors. But all this may be done with *these utensils*, if your *copper* be moveable. Make the boiler of *copper*, and not of sheet-iron, and fix it on a stand with a fire-place and stove-pipe; and then you have the whole to brew out of doors with as well as in-doors, which is a very great convenience.

58. Now, with regard to the *other scale* of brewing, little need be said; because, all the principles being the same, the utensils only are to be proportioned to the *quantity*. If only one sort of beer be to be brewed at a time, all the difference is, that, in order to extract the whole of the goodness of the malt, the mashing ought to be at *twice*. The two worts are then put together, and then you boil them together with the hops.

59. A Correspondent at *Morpeth* says, the whole of the utensils used by him are a twenty-gallon *pot*, a mashing-tub, that also answers for a tun-tub, and a shallow tub for a cooler; and that these are plenty for a person who is any thing of a contriver. This is very true; and these things will cost not more, perhaps, than *forty shillings*. A nine gallon cask of beer can be brewed very well with such utensils. Indeed, it is what used to be done by almost every labouring man in the kingdom, until the high price of malt and comparatively low price of wages rendered the people too poor and miserable to be able to brew at all. A Correspondent at Bristol has obligingly sent me the model of utensils for *brewing on a small scale;* but, as they consist chiefly of

brittle ware, I am of opinion, that they would not so well answer the purpose.

60. Indeed, as to the country labourers, all they want is the ability to *get the malt.* Mr. ELLMAN, in his evidence before the Agricultural Committee, said, that, when he began farming, forty-five years ago, there was not a labourer's family in the parish that did not brew their own beer and enjoy it by their own fire-sides ; and that, *now, not one single family did it, from want of ability to get the malt.* It is the *tax* that prevents their getting the malt ; for, the barley is cheap enough. The tax causes a monopoly in the hands of the maltsters, who, when the tax is *two and sixpence,* make the malt cost 7s. 6d. though the barley cost but 2s. 6d. ; and though the malt, tax and all, ought to cost but about 5s. 6d. If the tax were taken off, this *pernicious monopoly* would be destroyed.

61. The reader will easily see, that, in proportion to the quantity wanted to be brewed must be the size of the utensils ; but, I may observe here, that the above utensils are sufficient for three, or even four, bushels of malt, if stronger beer be wanted.

62. When it is necessary, in case of falling short in the quantity wanted to fill up the ale-cask, some may be taken from the small beer. But, upon the *whole brewing,* there ought to be no falling short; because, if the casks be not *filled up,* the beer will not be good, and certainly will not *keep.* Great care should be taken as to the *cleansing* of the

casks. They should be made perfectly *sweet;* or it is impossible to have good beer.

63. The cellar, for beer to keep any length of time, should be cool. Under *a hill* is the best place for a cellar; but, at any rate, a cellar of a good depth, and *dry.* At certain times of the year, beer that is kept long will ferment. The vent pegs must, in such cases, be loosened a little, and afterwards fastened.

64. Small-beer may be tapped almost directly. It is a sort of joke, that it should *see a Sunday;* but, that it may do before it be two days old. In short, any beer is better than water; but, it should have some strength and some *weeks* of age at any rate.

65. I cannot conclude this Essay, without expressing my ardent wish, that the Bill, which *Mr. Brougham* has promised to bring in to authorize the *general retail of Beer* will become a law. This really seems necessary to prevent the King's subjects from being *poisoned.* The Brewers and Porter Quacks have carried their tricks to such an extent, that there is *no safety* for those who drink Brewer's beer.

66. The best and most effectual thing is, however, for people to *brew their own beer*, to enable them and induce them to do which I have done all that lies in my power. A longer Treatise on the subject would have been of no use. These few plain directions will suffice for those who have a disposition to do the thing; and, those who have not, would remain unmoved by any thing that I could say.

67. There seems to be a *great number of things to do* in brewing; but, the greater part of them require only about a *minute* each. A brewing, such as I have given the detail of above, may be completed in *a day;* but, by the word *day* I mean to include the *morning*, beginning at four o'clock.

68. The putting of the beer into barrel is not more than an hour's work for a servant woman, or a tradesman's or farmer's wife. There is no *heavy* work, no work too heavy for a woman in any part of the business; otherwise I would not recommend it to be performed by the women, who, though so amiable in themselves, are never quite so amiable as when they are *useful;* and, as to beauty, though men may fall in love with girls *at play*, there is nothing to make them stand to their love like seeing them at *work*. In conclusion of these remarks on beer brewing, I once more express my most anxious desire to see abolished for ever the accursed tax on *malt*, which, I verily believe, has done more harm to the people of England than was ever done to any people by plague, pestilence, famine, and civil war.

69. In Paragraph 76, in Paragraph 108, and perhaps, in another place or two (of the last edition) I spoke of the *Machine* for brewing. The Work being *stereotyped*, it would have been troublesome to alter those Paragraphs; but, of course, the Public, in reading them, will bear in mind what has been *now* said relative to the *Machine*. The inventor of that Machine deserves great praise for his efforts to promote private brewing; and, as I said before, in certain confined situations, and where the beer is to be merely *small beer*, and for *immediate* use, and where *time* and *room* are of such importance as to make the *cost* of the Machine comparatively of trifling consideration, the Machine may, possibly, be found to be an useful utensil.

70. Having stated the inducements to the brewing of beer, and given the plainest directions that I was able to give for the doing of the thing, I shall, next, proceed to the subject of *Bread*. But, this subject is too large and of too much moment to be treated with brevity, and must, therefore, be put off till my next Number. I cannot, in the mean while, dismiss the subject of *Brewing Beer* without once more adverting to its many advantages, as set forth in the foregoing Number of this Work.

71. The following instructions for the making of *Porter* will clearly show what sort of stuff is sold at *public-houses* in London; and we may pretty fairly suppose, that the public-house beer in the country is not superior to it in quality. " A quarter of malt, " with these ingredients, will make *five barrels* o " *good porter*. Take one quarter of high-coloured " malt, eight pounds of hops, nine pounds of *treacle*, " eight pounds of *colour*, eight pounds of sliced " *liquorice-root*, two drams of *salt of tartar*, two " ounces of *Spanish-licorice*, and half an ounce of " *capsicum*." The author says, that he merely gives the ingredients, as *used by many persons*.

72. This extract is taken from a *book on brewing,* recently published in London. What a curious composition! What a mess of drugs! But, if the brewers *openly avow* this, what have we to expect from the *secret practices* of them, and the *retailers* of the article! When we know, that *Beer-doctor* and *Brewers'-druggist* are professions, practised as openly as those of *Bug-man* and *Rat-killer,* are we simple enough to suppose that the above-named are the *only* drugs that people swallow in those potions, which they call *pots of beer ?* Indeed we know the contrary ; for, scarcely a week passes without witnessing the detection of some greedy wretch, who has used, in making or in *doctoring* his beer, drugs, forbidden by the law. And, it is not many weeks since one of these was convicted, in the Court of Excise, for using potent and dangerous drugs, by the means of which, and a suitable quantity of water, he made *two butts of beer into three.* Upon this occasion, it appeared that no less than *ninety* of these worthies were in the habit of pursuing the same practices. The drugs are not unpleasant to the taste : they sting the palate : they give a present relish : they communicate a momentary exhilaration : but, they give no force to the body, which, on the contrary, they enfeeble, and, in many instances, with time, destroy ; producing diseases from which the drinker would otherwise have been free to the end of his days.

73. But, look again at the receipt for making

D

Porter. Here are *eight* bushels of malt to 180 gallons of beer; that is to say, 25 gallons from the bushel. Now, the malt is eight shillings a bushel, and allowing eight pounds of the very *best hops*, they will cost but a shilling a pound. The malt and hops, then, for the 180 gallons, cost but *seventy-two shillings;* that is to say, only a little more than *fourpence three farthings a gallon*, for stuff which is now retailed for *twenty pence a gallon!* If this be not an abomination, I should be glad to know what is. Even if the treacle, colour, and the drugs, be included, the cost is not *fivepence a gallon;* and, yet, not content with this enormous extortion, there are wretches, who resort to the use of other, and pernicious drugs, in order to increase their gains!

74. To provide against this dreadful evil there is, and there can be, no *law;* for, it is *created by the law.* The *law* it is, that imposes the enormous **tax** on the *malt* and *hops;* the *law* it is, that imposes the *licence tax*, and places the power of granting the licence at the discretion of persons appointed by the government; the law it is that checks, in this way, the private brewing, and that prevents *free and fair competition* in the selling of beer, and, as long as the *law* do these, it will in vain endeavour to prevent the people from being destroyed by slow poison.

75. Innumerable are the benefits that would arise from a repeal of the taxes on malt and on hops. Tippling houses might then be shut up with justice

and propriety. The Labourer, the Artisan, the Tradesman, the Landlord, all would instantly feel the benefit. But the *Landlord* more, perhaps, in this case, than any other member of the community. The four or five pounds a year which the day-lábourer now drizzles away in tea-messes, he would divide with the farmer, if he had untaxed beer. His wages would *fall*, and fall to his *advantage* too. The fall of wages would be not less than 40*l.* upon a hundred acres. Thus 40*l.* would go, in the end, a fourth, perhaps, to the farmer, and three-fourths to the Landlord. This is the kind of work to *reduce poor-rates*, and to restore *husbandry to prosperity*. Undertaken this work *must* be, and *performed too;* but whether we shall see this until the estates have passed away from the *present race* of Landlords, is a question which must be referred to *time.*

76. Surely we may hope, that, when the American farmers shall see this little Essay, they will begin seriously to think of leaving off the use of the liver-burning and palsy-producing *Spirits.* Their *climate*, indeed, is something : *extremely hot* in one part of the year, and *extremely cold* in the other part of it. Nevertheless, they may have, and do have, very good beer if they will. *Negligence* is the greatest impediment in their way. I like the Americans very much ; and that, if there were no other, would be a reason for my not hiding their faults.

D 2

MAKING BREAD.

77. LITTLE time need be spent in dwelling on the necessity of *this* article to all families ; though, on account of the modern custom of using *potatoes* to supply the place of *bread*, it seems necessary to say a few words here on a subject, which, in another work, I have so amply, and, I think, so triumphantly discussed. I am the more disposed to revive the subject for a moment, in this place, from having read, in the Evidence recently given before the Agricultural Committee, that many labourers, especially in the West of England, use potatoes *instead* of bread to a very great extent. And I find, from the same evidence, that it is the custom to allot to labourers " *a potatoe ground* " in part-payment of their wages ! This has a tendency to bring English labourers down to the state of the Irish, whose mode of living, as to food, is but one remove from that of the pig, and of the ill-fed pig too.

78. I was, in reading the above-mentioned Evidence, glad to find, that Mr. EDWARD WAKEFIELD, the best informed and most candid of all the witnesses, gave it as his opinion, that the increase which had taken place in the cultivation of potatoes was " *injurious to the country ;*" an opinion, which must, I think, be adopted by every one who takes the trouble to reflect a little upon the subject. For, leaving out of the question, the slovenly and beastly habits engendered amongst the labouring classes by constantly lifting their principal food at once out f the earth to their mouths, by eating without the necessity of any implements other than the hands and the teeth, and by dispensing with every thing requiring skill in the preparation of the food and requiring cleanliness in its consumption or preservation; leaving these out of the question, though they are all matters of great moment, when we consider their effects in the rearing of a family, we shall find, that, in mere quantity of food; that is to say, of *nourishment*, bread is the preferable diet.

79. An acre of land, that will produce 300 bushels of potatoes, will produce 32 bushels of wheat. I state this as an average fact, and am not at all afraid of being contradicted by any one well acquainted with husbandry. The potatoes are supposed to be of a *good sort*, as it is called, and the wheat may be supposed to weigh 60 pounds a bushel. It is a fact clearly established, that, after the *water*, the *stringy* substance, and the *earth*, are taken from the potatoe, there remains only one *tenth* of the rough raw weight of nutritious matter, or matter which is deemed equally nutritious with bread, and, as the raw potatoes weigh 56 lb. a bushel, the acre will yield 1,830 lb. of nutritious matter. Now mind, a bushel of wheat, weighing 60lb. will make of *household bread* (that is to say, taking out only the *bran*) 65 lb

Thus, the acre yields 2,080 lb. of bread. As to the *expenses*, the seed and act of planting are about equal in the two cases. But, while the potatoes *must* have cultivation during their growth, the wheat needs none; and while the wheat straw is worth from three to five pounds an acre, the haulm of the potatoes is not worth one single truss of that straw. Then, as to the expense of gathering, housing, and keeping the potatoe crop, it is enormous, besides the risk of loss by frost, which may be safely taken, on an average, at a tenth of the crop. Then comes the expense of *cooking*. The thirty-two bushels of wheat, supposing a bushel to be baked at a time (which would be the case in a large family) would demand *thirty-two heatings of the oven*. Suppose a bushel of potatoes to be cooked every day in order to supply the place of this bread, then we have *nine hundred boilings of the pot*; unless *cold potatoes* be eaten at some of the meals; and, in that case, the diet must be *cheering* indeed! Think of the *labour;* think of the *time;* think of all the peelings and scrapings and washings and messings attending these *nine hundred boilings of the pot!* For it must be a considerable time before English people can be brought to eat potatoes in the Irish style; that is to say, scratch them out of the earth with their paws, toss them into a pot without washing, and when boiled, turn them out upon a dirty board, and then sit round that board, peel the skin and dirt from one at a time and eat the inside. Mr. Curwen was delighted with "*Irish hospitality*," because the people there receive no parish relief; upon which I can only say, that I wish him the exclusive benefit of such hospitality.

80. I have here spoken of a large quantity of each of the sorts of food. I will now come to a comparative view, more immediately applicable to a labourer's family. When wheat is *ten* shillings the bushel, potatoes, bought at best hand (I am speaking of the country generally) are about *two* shillings a bushel. Last Spring the average price of wheat might be *six and sixpence;* and the average price of potatoes (in small quantities) was about *eighteen pence;* though, by the wagon load, I saw potatoes bought at a *shilling* a bushel, to give to sheep; then, observe, these were of the coarsest kind, and the farmer had to fetch them at a considerable expense, I think, therefore, that I give the advantage to the potatoes when I say that they sell, upon an average, for full a *fifth* part as much as the wheat sells for, per bushel, while they contain four pounds less weight than the bushel of wheat; while they yield only five pounds and a half of nutritious matter equal to bread; and while the bushel of wheat will yield *sixty-five pounds of bread*, besides the ten pounds of bran. Hence it is clear, that, instead of that *saving*, which is everlastingly dinned in our ears, from the use of potatoes, there is a *waste of more than one half;* seeing that, when wheat is *ten shillings* the bushel, you can have *sixty-five pounds of bread for*

the ten shillings; and can have out of potatoes only five pounds and a half of nutritious matter equal to bread for *two shillings!* This being the case, I trust, that we shall soon hear no more of those *savings*, which the labourer makes by the use of potatoes; I hope we shall, in the words of DOCTOR DRENNEN, "leave Ireland to her *lazy* root," if she choose still to adhere to it. It is the root, also, of slovenliness, filth, misery, and slavery; its cultivation has increased in England with the increase of the paupers: both, I thank God, are upon the decline. Englishmen seem to be upon the return to beer and bread, from water and potatoes; and, therefore, I shall now proceed to offer some observations to the Cottager, calculated to induce him to bake his own bread.

81. As I have before stated, sixty pounds of wheat, that is to say, where the Winchester bushel weighs sixty pounds, will make sixty-five pounds of bread, besides the leaving of about ten pounds of bran. This is household bread, made of flour from which the bran only is taken. If you make fine flour, you take out pollard, as they call it, as well as bran, and then you have a smaller quantity of bread and a greater quantity of offal; but, even of this finer bread, bread equal in fineness to the baker's bread, you get from *fifty-eight to fifty-nine* pounds out of the bushel of wheat. Now, then, let us see how many quartern loaves you get out of the bushel of wheat, supposing it to be fine flour, in the first place. You get thirteeen quartern loaves and a

half; these cost you, at the present average price of wheat (seven and sixpence a bushel), in the first place 7s. 6d.; then 3d. for yeast; then not more than 3d. for grinding; because you have about thirteen pounds of offal, which is worth more than a $\frac{1}{2}d$. a pound, while the grinding is 9d. a bushel. Thus, then, the bushel of bread of fifty-nine pounds cost you *eight shillings;* and it yields you the weight of thirteen and a half quartern loaves. These quartern loaves *now* (Dec. 1821.) sell at Kensington, at the baker's shop, at 1s. $\frac{1}{2}d.$; that is to say, the thirteen quartern loaves and a half cost 14s. $7\frac{1}{2}d.$ I omitted to mention the salt, which would cost you 4d. more. So that, here is 6s. $3\frac{1}{2}d.$ saved upon the baking of a bushel of bread. The baker's quartern loaf is indeed cheaper in the country than at Kensington, by, probably, a penny in the loaf; which would still, however, leave a saving of 5s. upon the bushel of bread. But, besides this, pray think a little of the materials of which the baker's loaf is composed. The *alum,* the *ground potatoes,* and other materials, it being a notorious fact, that the bakers, in London at least, have *mills,* wherein to grind their potatoes; so large is the scale upon which they use that material. It is probable, that, out of a bushel of wheat, they make between *sixty* and *seventy* pounds of bread, though they have no more *flour,* and, of course, no more nutritious matter, than you have in your fifty-nine pounds of bread. But, at the least, supposing their bread to be as good as yours in quality, you have,

D 5

allowing a shilling for the heating of the oven, a clear 4s. saved upon every bushel of bread. If you consume half a bushel a week, that is to say, about a quartern loaf a day, this is a saving of 5l. 4s. a year, or full a sixth part, if not a fifth part, of the earnings of a labourer in husbandry.

82. How wasteful, then, and, indeed, how shameful, for a labourer's wife to go to the baker's shop; and how negligent, how criminally careless of the welfare of his family, must the labourer be, who permits so scandalous an use of the proceeds of his labour! But I have, hitherto, taken a view of the matter the least possibly advantageous to the home-baked bread. For, ninety-nine times out of a hundred, the fuel for heating the oven costs very little. The hedgers, the copsers, the woodmen of all descriptions, have fuel for little or nothing. At any rate, to heat the oven cannot, upon an average, take the Country through, cost the labourer more than 6d. a bushel. Then, again, fine flour need not ever be used, and ought not to be used. This adds six pounds of bread to the bushel, or nearly another quartern loaf and a half, making nearly fifteen quartern loaves out of the bushel of wheat. The finest flour is by no means the most wholesome; and, at any rate, there is more nutritious matter in a pound of household bread, than in a pound of baker's bread. Besides this, rye, and even barley, especially when mixed with wheat, make very good bread. Few people upon the face of the earth live better than

the Long Islanders. Yet, nine families out of ten, seldom eat wheaten bread. Rye is the flour that they principally make use of. Now, rye is seldom more than two-thirds the price of wheat, and barley is seldom more than half the price of wheat. Half rye and half wheat, taking out a little more of the offal, make very good bread. Half wheat, a quarter rye and a quarter barley; nay, one-third of each, make bread that I could be very well content to live upon all my lifetime; and, even barley alone; if the barley be good, and none but the finest flour taken out of it, has in it, measure for measure, ten times the nutrition of potatoes. Indeed the fact is well known, that our forefathers used barley bread to a very great extent. Its only fault, with those who dislike it, is its sweetness, a fault which we certainly have not to find with the baker's loaf, which has in it, little more of the *sweetness* of grain than is to be found in the offal which comes from the sawings of deal boards. The nutritious nature of barley is amply proved by the effect, and very rapid effect of its meal, in the fatting of hogs and of poultry of all descriptions. They will fatten quicker upon meal of barley than upon any other thing. The flesh, too, is sweeter than that proceeding from any other food, with the exception of that which proceeds from *buck wheat*, a grain little used in England. That proceeding from Indian corn is, indeed, still sweeter and finer, but this is wholly out of the question with us.

83. I am, by and by, to speak of the *cow* to be kept by the labourer in husbandry. Then there will be *milk* to wet the bread with, an exceedingly great improvement in its taste as well as in its quality! This, of all the ways of using skim milk, is the most advantageous; and, this great advantage must be wholly thrown away, if the bread of the family be bought at the shop. With milk, bread with very little wheat in it, may be made far better than baker's bread; and, leaving the milk out of the question, taking a third of each sort of grain, you would get bread weighing as much as fourteen quartern loaves, for about 5*s*. 9*d*. at present prices of grain; that is to say, you would get it for about 5*d*. the quartern loaf, all expenses included; thus you have nine pounds and ten ounces of bread a day for about 5*s*. 9*d*. a week. Here is enough for a very large family. Very few labourers' families can want so much as this, unless indeed there be several persons in it capable of earning something by their daily labour. Here is cut and come again. Here is bread always for the table. Bread to carry a field; always a hunch of bread ready to put into the hand of a hungry child. We hear a great deal about " *children crying for bread*," and objects of compassion they and their parents are, when the latter have not the means of obtaining a sufficiency of bread. But I should be glad to be informed, how it is possible for a labouring man, who earns, upon an average, 10*s*. a week, who has not more than four

children (and if he have more some ought to be doing
something) ; who has a garden of a quarter of an
acre of land (for that makes part of my plan) ; who
has a wife as industrious as she ought to be ; who
does not waste his earnings at the alehouse or the
tea shop : I should be glad to know how such a man,
while wheat shall be at the price of about 6s. a bushel,
can possibly have children crying for bread !

84. Cry, indeed, they must if he will persist in
giving thirteen shillings for a bushel of bread instead
of 5s. 9d. Such a man is not to say that the bread
which I have described is *not good enough.* It was
good enough for his forefathers, who were too proud
to be paupers, that is to say, abject and willing slaves.
" Hogs eat barley." And hogs will eat wheat, too,
when they can get at it. Convicts in condemned
cells eat wheaten bread ; but we think it no degradation to eat wheaten bread, too. I am for depriving
the labourer of none of his rights ; I would have him
oppressed in no manner or shape ; I would have him
bold and free ; but to have him such, he must have
bread in his house, sufficient for all his family, and
whether that bread be fine or coarse must depend
upon the different circumstances which present
themselves in the cases of different individuals.

85. The married man has no right to expect the
same plenty of food and of raiment that the single
man has. The time before marriage is the time to
lay by, or, if the party choose, to indulge himself in
the absence of labour. To marry is a voluntary

act, and it is attended in the result, with great pleasures and advantages. If, therefore, the laws be fair and equal ; if the state of things be such, that a labouring man can, with the usual ability of labourers, and with constant industry, care and sobriety ; with decency of deportment towards all his neighbours, cheerful obedience to his employer, and a due subordination to the laws : if the state of things be such, that such a man's earnings be sufficient to maintain himself and family with food, raiment, and lodging needful for them ; such man has no reason to complain ; and no labouring man has reason to complain, if the numerousness of his family should call upon him for extraordinary exertion, or for frugality uncommonly rigid. The man with a large family has, if it be not in a great measure his own fault, a greater number of pleasures and of blessings than other men. If he be wise, and *just* as well as wise, he will see that it is reasonable for him to expect less delicate fare than his neighbours, who have a less number of children or no children at all. He will see the justice as well as the necessity of his resorting to the use of coarser bread, and thus, endeavour to make up that, or, at least, a part of that which he loses in comparison with his neighbours. The quality of the bread ought, in every case, to be proportioned to the number of the family and the means of the head of that family. Here is no injury to health proposed ; but, on the contrary, the best security for its preservation. Without bread, all is misery.

The Scripture truly calls it the staff of life; and it may be called, too, the pledge of peace and happiness in the labourer's dwelling.

86. As to the act of making bread, it would be shocking indeed, if that had to be taught by the means of books. Every woman, high or low, ought to know how to make bread. If she do not, she is unworthy of trust and confidence; and, indeed, a mere burthen upon the community. Yet, it is but too true, that many women, even amongst those who have to get their living by their labour, know nothing of the making of bread; and seem to understand little more about it than the part which belongs to its consumption. A Frenchman, a Mr. Cusar, who had been born in the West Indies, told me, that till he came to Long Island, he never knew *how the flour came*; that he was surprised when he learnt that it was squeezed out of little grains that grew at the tops of straw; for that he had always had an idea that it was got out of some large substances, like the yams that grow in tropical climates. He was a very sincere and good man, and I am sure he told me truth. And this may be the more readily believed, when we see so many women in England, who seem to know no more of the constituent parts of a loaf than they know of those of the Moon. Servant women in abundance appear to think that loaves are made by the baker, as knights are made by the king; things of their pure creation, a creation, too, in which no one else can participate. Now, is not this an

enormous evil? And whence does it come? Servant women are the children of the labouring classes; and they would all know how to make bread, and know well how to make it too, if they had been fed on bread of their mother's and their own making.

87. How serious a matter, then, is this, even in this point of view! A servant that cannot make bread is not entitled to the same wages as one that can. If she can neither bake nor brew; if she be ignorant of the nature of flour, yeast, malt and hops, what is she good for? If she understand these matters well; if she be able to supply her employer with bread and with beer; she is really *valuable;* she is entitled to good wages, and to consideration and respect into the bargain; but if she be wholly deficient in these particulars, and can merely dawdle about with a bucket and a broom, she can be of very little consequence: to lose her is merely to lose a consumer of food, and she can expect very little indeed in the way of desire to make her life easy and pleasant. Why should any one have such desire? She is not a child of the family. She is not a relation. Any one as well as she can take in a loaf from the baker, or a barrel of beer from the brewer. She has nothing whereby to bind her employer to her. To sweep a room any thing is capable of that has got two hands. In short, she has no useful skill, no useful ability, she is an ordinary drudge, and she is treated accordingly.

88. But, if such be her state in the house of an

employer, what is her state in the house of a *husband?*
The lover is blind ; but the husband has eyes to see
with. He soon discovers that there is something
wanted besides dimples and cherry cheeks ; and I
would have fathers seriously to reflect, and to be well
assured, that, the way to make their daughters to
be long admired, beloved and respected by their
husbands, is to make them skilful, able and active in
the most necessary concerns of a family. Eating
and drinking come three times every day; the pre-
parations for these, and all the ministry necessary to
them belong to the wife, and I hold it to be impossible,
that, at the end of two years, a really ignorant,
sluttish wife, should possess any thing worthy of the
name of love from her husband. This, therefore, is a
matter of far greater moment to the father of a
family, than, whether the Parson of the parish, or the
Methodist Priest, be the most " *Evangelical* " of the
two ; for, it is here a question of the daughter's happiness or misery for life. And I have no hesitation
to say, that if I were a labouring man, I should prefer
teaching my daughters to bake, brew, milk, make
butter and cheese, to teaching them to read the Bible
till they had got every word of it by heart; and I
should think, too, nay I should know, that I was in
the former case doing my duty towards God as well
as towards my children.

89. When we see a family of dirty, ragged little
creatures, let us inquire into the cause: and ninety-
nine times out of every hundred we shall find, that

the parents themselves have been brought up in the same way. But a consideration which ought of itself to be sufficient, is the contempt in which a husband will naturally hold a wife that is ignorant of the matters necessary to the conducting of a family. A woman who understands all the things above mentioned is really a skilful person ; a person worthy of respect, and that will be treated with respect, too, by all but brutish employers or brutish husbands; and such, though sometimes, are not very frequently found. Besides, if natural justice and our own interests had not the weight which they have, such valuable persons will be treated with respect. They know their own worth; and, accordingly, they are more careful of their character, more careful not to lessen by misconduct the value which they possess from their skill and ability.

90. Thus, then, the interest of the labourer; his health ; the health of his family ; the peace and happiness of his home; the prospects of his children through life; their skill, their ability, their habits of cleanliness, and even their moral deportment ; all combine to press upon him the adoption and the constant practice of this branch of domestic economy. " Can she *bake?*" Is the question that I always put. If she can, she is *worth a pound or two a year more.* Is that nothing.? Is it nothing for a labouring man to make his four or five daughters worth eight or ten pounds a year more ; and that, too, while he is by the same means providing the more plentifully for

himself and the rest of his family? The reasons on the side of the thing that I contend for are endless; but if this one motive be not sufficient, I am sure all that I have said, and all that I could say, must be wholly unavailing.

91. Before, however, I dismiss this subject, let me say a word or two to those persons, who do not come under the denomination of labourers. In London, or in any very large Town, where the space is so confined, and where the proper fuel is not handily to be come at and stored for use, to bake your own bread may be attended with too much difficulty; but, in all other situations there appears to me to be hardly any excuse for not baking bread at home. If the family consist of twelve or fourteen persons, the money actually saved in this way (even at present prices) would be little short of from twenty to thirty pounds a year. At the utmost here is only the time of one woman occupied, one day in the week. Now mind, here are twenty-five pounds to be employed in some way different from that of giving it to a baker. If you add five of these pounds to a woman's wages, is not that full as well employed as giving it in wages to the baker's men? Is it not better employed for you? and is it not better employed for the community? It is very certain, that, if the practice were as prevalent as I could wish, there would be a large deduction from the regular baking population; but, would there be any harm if less alum were imported into England, and if some of those youths were left

at the plough, who are now bound in apprenticeships
to learn the art and mystery of doing that which
every girl in the kingdom ought to be taught to do by
her mother? It ought to be a maxim with every
Master and every Mistress, never to employ another
to do that which can be done as well by their own
servants. The more of their money that is retained
in the hands of their own people, the better it is for
them all together. Besides, a man of a right mind
must be pleased with the reflection, that there is a
great mass of skill and ability under his own roof.
He feels stronger and more independent on this
account, all pecuniary advantage out of the question.
It is impossible to conceive any thing more con-
temptible than a crowd of men and women living
together in a house, and constantly looking out of it
for people to bring them food and drink, and to fetch
their garments to and fro. Such a crowd resemble
a nest of unfledged birds, absolutely dependent for
their very existence on the activity and success of
the old ones.

92. Yet, on men go, from year to year, in this state
of wretched dependence, even when they have all
the means of living within themselves, which is certainly the happiest state of life that any one can
enjoy. It may be asked, where is the mill to be
found? where is the wheat to be got? The answer
is, where is there not a mill? where is there not a
market? They are every where, and the difficulty
is to discover what can be the particular attractions

contained in that long and luminous manuscript, a baker's half-yearly bill.

93. With regard to the Mill, in speaking of families of any considerable number of persons, the mill has, with me, been more than once a subject of observation in print. I for a good while experienced the great inconvenience and expense of sending my wheat and other grain to be ground at a mill. This expense, in case of a considerable family, living at only a mile from a mill, is something; but the inconvenience and uncertainty, are great. In my " Year's Residence in America," from paragraphs 1031 and onwards, I give an account of a horse-mill, which I had in my farm yard; and I showed, I think very clearly, that corn could be ground cheaper in this way than by wind or water, and that it would answer well to grind for sale in this way as well as for home use. Since my return to England I have seen a mill, erected in consequence of what the owner had read in my book. This mill belongs to a small farmer, who, when he cannot work on his land with his horses, or, in the season when he has little for them to do, grinds wheat, sells the flower; and he takes in grists to grind, as other millers do. This mill goes with three small horses; but, what I would recommend to gentlemen with considerable families, or to farmers, is a mill, such as I myself have at present.

94. With this mill, turned by a man and a stout boy, I can grind six bushels of wheat in a day, and dress the flour. The grinding of six bushels of wheat

at ninepence a bushel comes to four and sixpence, which pays the man and the boy, supposing them (which is not and seldom can be the case) to be hired for the express purpose, out of the street. With the same mill you grind meat for your pigs; and of this you will get eight or ten bushels ground in a day. You have no trouble about sending to the mill; you are sure to have your *own wheat*; for, strange as it may seem, I used sometimes to find that I sent white Essex wheat to the mill, and that it brought me flour from very coarse red wheat. There is no accounting for this, except by supposing that wind and water power has something in it to change the very nature of the grain; as, when I came to grind by horses, such as the wheat went into the hopper, so the flour came out into the bin.

95. But mine now is only on the petty scale of providing for a dozen of persons and a small lot of pigs. For a farm-house, or a gentleman's house in the country, where there would be *room* to have a walk for a horse, you might take the labour from the men, clap any little horse, pony, or even ass to the wheel; and he would grind you off eight or ten bushels of wheat in a day, and both he and you would have the thanks of your men into the bargain.

96. The cost of this Mill is twenty-pounds. The Dresser is four more; the horse-path and wheel might, possibly, be four or five more; and I am very certain, that to any farmer living at a mile from a mill (and that is less than the average distance

perhaps); having twelve persons in family; having forty pigs to feed and twenty hogs to fatten, the savings of such a mill would pay the whole expenses of it the very first year. Such a farmer cannot send less than *fifty times* a year to the mill. Think of that, in the first place! The elements are not always propitious: sometimes the water fails, and sometimes the wind. Many a farmer's wife has been tempted to vent her spleen on both. At best, there must be horse and man or boy, and, perhaps, cart, to go to the mill; and that, too, observe, in all weathers, and in the harvest as well as at other times of the year. The case is one of imperious necessity: neither floods nor droughts, nor storms nor calms, will allay the cravings of the kitchen, nor quiet the clamorous uproar of the stye. Go, somebody must, to some place or other, and back they must come with flour and with meal. One summer many persons came down the country more than fifty miles to a mill that I knew in Pennsylvania; and I have known farmers in England, carry their grists more than fifteen miles to be ground. It is surprising, that, under these circumstances, hand-mills and horse-mills should not, long ago, have become of more general use; especially when one considers that the labour, in this case, would cost the farmer next to nothing. To grind would be the work of a wet day. There is no farmer, who does not, at least fifty days in every year, exclaim, when he gets up in the morning, " What shall I set *them* at to-day !" If he had a mill, he would make them pull off their shoes, sweep all out clean, winnow up some corn, if he had it not already done, and grind and dress, and have every thing in order. No scolding within doors about the grist ; no squeaking in the stye ; no boy sent off in the rain to the mill.

97. But, there is one advantage which I have not yet mentioned, and which is the greatest of all ; namely, that you would have the power of supplying your married labourers, your blacksmith's men sometimes, your wheelwright's men at other times; and, indeed, the greater part of the persons that you employed, with good flour, instead of their going to purchase this flour, after it had passed through the hands of a Corn Merchant, a Miller, a Flour Merchant, and a Huckster, every one of whom, does and must, have a profit out of the flour, arising from wheat grown upon, and sent away from, your very farm ! I used to let all my people have flour at the same price that they would otherwise have been compelled to give for worse flour. *Every Farmer* will understand me when I say, that he ought to pay for nothing in *money,* which he can pay for in any thing but money. His maxim is to keep the money that he takes, as long as he can. Now here is a most effectual way of putting that maxim in practice to a very great extent. Farmers know well that it is the Saturday night which empties their pockets; and here is the means of cutting off a good half of the Saturday night. The men have better flour for the

same money, and still the Farmer keeps at home, those profits which would go to the maintaining of the Dealers in wheat and in flour.

98. The maker of my little mill is Mr. HILL, of Oxford-street. The expense is what I have stated it to be. I, with my small establishment, find the thing convenient, and advantageous; what then must it be to a gentleman, in the country, who has room and horses, and a considerable family to provide for. The Dresser is so contrived as to give you at once, meal, of four degrees of fineness; so that, for certain purposes, you may take the very finest; and indeed, you may have your flour, and your bread of course, of what degree of fineness you please. But, there is also a *steel-mill*, much less *expensive*, requiring *less labour*, and yet quite sufficient for *a family*. Mills of this sort, very good and at a reasonable price, are to be had of Mr. PARKES, in *Fenchurch-street*, London. These are very complete things of their kind. Mr. PARKES, has, also excellent Malt-Mills.

99. In concluding this part of my Treatise, I cannot help expressing my hope of being instrumental in inducing a part of the labourers, at any rate, to bake their own bread; and, above all things, to abandon the use of " Ireland's *lazy* root." Nevertheless, so extensive is the erroneous opinion relative to this villainous root, that I really began to despair of checking its cultivation and use, till I saw the declaration, which Mr. WAKEFIELD had the good

E

sense and the spirit to make before the "AGRICUL-
TURAL COMMITTEE." Be it observed, too, that Mr.
WAKEFIELD had, himself, made a survey of the
state of Ireland. What he saw there did not encou-
rage him, doubtless, to be an advocate for the growing of this root of wretchedness. It is an undeniable
fact, that, in the proportion that this root is in use,
as a *substitute for bread*, the people are wretched;
the reasons for which I have explained and inforced,
a hundred times over. Mr. WILLIAM HANNING told
the Committee that the labourers in his part of
Somersetshire were " almost wholly supplied with
" potatoes, *breakfast* and *dinner*, brought them *in*
" *the fields,* and nothing but potatoes; and that they
" used, in better times, to get a certain portion of
" bacon and cheese, which, on account of their
" poverty, they do not eat now." It is impossible
that men can be *contented* in such a state of things:
it is unjust to desire them to be contented: it is a
state of misery and degradation to which no part of
any community can have any show of right to reduce another part: men so degraded have no protection; and it is a disgrace to form part of a community to which they belong. This degradation has
been occasioned by a silent change in the value of
the money of the country. This has purloined the
wages of the labourer; it has reduced him by degrees to housel with the spider and the bat and to
feed with the pig. It has changed the habits and, in
a great measure, the character, of the people. The

sins of this terrible system are enormous and unde-
scribable; but, thank God! they seem to be approaching to their end! Money is resuming its value,
labour is recovering its price; let us hope that the
wretched potatoe is disappearing, and that, we shall,
once more, see the knife in the labourer's hand and
the loaf upon his board.

[This was written in 1821. *Now* (1823) we have
had the experience of 1822, when, for the first time,
the world saw a considerable part of a people,
plunged into all the horrors of *famine*, at a moment
when the government of that nation declared *food to
be too abundant!* Yes, the year 1822, saw Ireland
in this state; saw the people of whole parishes
receiving the *extreme unction* preparatory to yielding
up their breath for want of food; and this, while
large exports of meat and flour were taking place in
that country! But, horrible as this was, disgraceful
as it was to the name of Ireland, it was attended with
this good effect: it brought out, from many Members
of Parliament (in their places), and from the public
in general, the acknowledgment, that the *misery* and
degradation of the Irish were chiefly owing to the *use
of the potatoe as the almost sole food of the people.*]

100. In my next Number I shall treat of the *keeping of cows*. I have said that I will teach the Cottager how to keep a cow all the year round upon
the produce of a quarter of an acre, or, in other
words, *forty rods*, of land; and, in my next, I will
make good my promise.

E 2

No. IV.

MAKING BREAD.

(Continued.)

101. IN the last Number, at paragraph 86, I observed, that I hoped it was unnecessary for me to give any directions as to the mere *act* of making bread. But, several co respondents inform me, that, without these directions, a conviction of the utility of baking bread at home is of *no use to them.* Therefore, I shall here give those directions, receiving my instructions here from one, who, I thank God, does know how to perform this act.

102. Suppose the quantity be a bushel of flour. Put this flour into a *trough* that people have for the purpose, or, it may be in a clean smooth tub of any shape, if not too deep, and if sufficiently large. Make a pretty deep hole in the middle of this heap of flour. Take (for a bushel) a pint of good fresh yeast, mix it and stir it well up in a pint of *soft* water milk-warm. Pour this into the hole in the heap of flour. Then take a spoon and work it round the outside of this body of moisture so as to bring into that body, by degrees, flour enough to make it form a *thin batter,* which you must stir about well for a minute or two. Then take a handful of flour and scatter it thinly over the head of this batter, so as to *hide* it. Then cover the whole over with a cloth to keep it *warm ;* and this covering, as well as the situation of the trough as to distance from the fire must depend on the nature of

the place and state of the weather as to heat and cold. When you perceive that the batter has risen enough to make *cracks* in the flour that you covered it over with, you begin to form the whole mass into *dough*, thus : you begin round the hole containing the batter, working the flour into the batter, and pouring in, as it is wanted to make the flour mix with the batter, soft water milk-warm, or milk, as hereafter to be mentioned. Before you begin this, you scatter the *salt* over the heap at the rate of *half a pound* to a bushel of flour. When you have got the whole *sufficiently moist*, you *knead it well*. This is a grand part of the business ; for, unless the dough be *well worked*, there will be *little round lumps of flour in the loaves;* and, besides, the original batter, which is to give fermentation to the whole, will not be duly mixed. The dough must, therefore, be well worked. The *fists* must go heartily into it. It must be rolled over ; pressed out ; folded up and pressed out again, until it be completely mixed, and formed into a *stiff* and *tough dough*. This is *labour*, mind. I have never quite liked baker's bread since I saw a great heavy fellow, in a bake-house in France, kneading bread with his *naked feet !* His feet looked very *white* to be sure : whether they were of that colour *before he got into the trough* I could not tell. God forbid, that I should suspect that this is ever done *in England !* It is *labour;* but, what is *exercise* other than labour ? Let a young woman bake a bushel once a week, and she will do very well without phials and gallipots.

103. Thus, then, the dough is made. And, when made, it is to be formed into a lump in the middle of the trough, and, with a little dry flour thinly scattered over it, covered over again to be kept warm and to ferment; and in this state, if all be done rightly, it will not have to remain more than about 15 or 20 minutes.

104. In the mean while *the oven is to be heated;* and this is much more than half the art of the operation. When an oven is properly heated can be known only by *actual observation.* Women who understand the matter, know when the heat is right the moment they put their faces within a yard of the oven-mouth; and, once or twice observing is enough for any person of common capacity. But this much may be said in the way of *rule:* that the fuel (I am supposing a brick oven) should be *dry* (not *rotten*) wood, and not mere *brush*-wood, but rather *fagot-sticks.* If larger wood, it ought to be split up into sticks not more than two, or two and a half, inches through. Brush-wood that is *strong*, not green and not too old, if it be hard in its nature and has some *sticks* in it may do. The *woody* parts of furze, or ling, will heat an oven very well. But, the thing is, to have a *lively* and yet *somewhat strong* fire; so that the oven may be heated in about 15 minutes, and retain its heat sufficiently long.

105. The oven should be hot by the time that the dough, as mentioned in paragraph 103, has remained in the lump about 20 minutes. When both are

ready, take out the fire and wipe the oven out clean, and, at nearly about the same moment, take the dough out upon the lid of the baking trough, or some proper place, cut it up into pieces, and make it up into loaves, kneading it again in these separate parcels ; and, as you go on, shaking a little flour over your board, to prevent the dough from adhering to it. The loaves should be put into the oven as *quickly* as possible after they are formed ; when in, the oven-lid, or door, should be fastened up *very closely;* and, if all be properly managed, loaves of about the size of quartern loaves, will be sufficiently baked in about *two hours.* But, they usually take down the *lid,* and *look* at the bread, in order to see how it is going on.

107. And, what is there, worthy of the name of *plague,* or *trouble,* in all this ? Here is no dirt, no filth, no rubbish, no *litter,* no *slop.* And, pray, what can be pleasanter to *behold ?* Talk, indeed, of your pantomimes and gaudy shows ; your processions and installations and coronations! Give me, for a beautiful sight, a neat and smart woman, heating her oven and setting in her bread! And, if the bustle does make the sign of labour glisten on her brow, where is the man that would not kiss that off, rather than lick the plaster from the cheek of a duchess ?

107. And, what is the *result ?* Why, good, wholesome food, sufficient for a considerable family for a week, prepared in three or four hours. T get this quantity of food, fit to be *eaten,* in the shape of potatoes, *how many fires !* What a washing, what a boil-

ing, what a peeling, what a slopping and what a
messing! The cottage everlastingly in a litter; the
woman's hands everlastingly wet and dirty; the children grimed up to the eyes with dust fixed on by
potatoe-starch; and ragged as colts, the poor mother's
time all being devoted to the everlasting boilings of
of the pot! Can any man, who knows any thing of
the labourer's life, deny this? And will, then, any
body, except the old shuffle-breeches band of the
Quarterly Review, who have, all their lives been
moving from garret to garret, who have seldom seen
the sun, and never the dew except in print; will any
body except these men say, that the people ought to
be taught to use potatoes as a *substitute for bread!*

BREWING BEER.

108. This matter has been fully treated of in the
two first Numbers. But, several correspondents,
wishing to fall upon some means of rendering the
practice beneficial to those who are *unable to purchase* brewing utensils, have recommended the
lending of them, or letting them out, round a neighbourhood. Another correspondent has, therefore,
pointed out to me *an act of parliament* which
touches upon this subject; and, indeed, what of
Excise Laws and Custom Laws and Combination Laws and Libel Laws, a human being in this

country scarcely knows what he dares do or what he dares say. What father, for instance, would have imagined, that, having brewing utensils, which two men can carry from house to house as easily as they can a basket, *he dared not lend them to his son, living in the next street, or at the next door ?* Yet such really is the law; for according to the Act, 5th of the 22 and 23 of that honest and sincere gentleman, Charles II. there is a penalty of 50*l.* for lending or letting brewing utensils. However, it has this limit; that the penalty is confined to *Cities, Corporate Towns* and *Market Towns*, WHERE THERE IS A PUBLIC BREW-HOUSE. So that, in the first place, you may let, or lend, in *any* place where there is *no public brew-house;* and, in all towns not *corporate* or *market,* and in all villages, hamlets and scattered places.

109. Another thing is, can a man, who has brewed beer at his own house in the country, bring that beer into town to his own house and for the use of his family there ? This has been asked of me. I cannot give a positive answer without reading about *seven large volumes in quarto of taxing laws.* The best way would be to *try it;* and, if any penalty, pay it by *subscription,* if that would not come under the law of *conspiracy !* However, I *think,* there can be no danger here. So monstrous a thing as this can, surely, not exist. If there be such a law, it is daily violated; for nothing is more common than for country gentlemen, who have a dislike to die by

E 5

poison, bringing their home-brewed beer to London.

110. Another correspondent recommends *parishes to make their own malt.* But, surely, the landlords mean to get rid of the *malt and salt tax!* Many dairies, I dare say, pay 50*l.* a year each in salt tax. How, then, are they to contend against Irish butter and Dutch butter and cheese? And, as to the malt tax, it is a dreadful drain from the land. I have heard of labourers, living in " *unkent places,*" making their *own malt,* even now! Nothing is so easy as to make your own malt, if you were permitted. You soak the barley about three days (according to the state of the weather) ; and then you put it upon stones or bricks, and *keep it turned,* till the root *shoots out;* and, then, to know when to *stop,* and to put it to dry, take up a corn (which you will find nearly transparent), and look through the skin of it. You will see the *spear,* that is to say, the shoot that would come out of the ground, pushing on towards the *point* of the barley-corn. It starts from the bottom, where the root comes out; and it goes on towards the other end; and would, if *kept moist,* come out at that other end when the root was about an inch long. So that, when you have got the *root to start* by soaking and turning in heap, the spear is *on its way.* If you look in through the skin, you will see it ; and, now observe ; when the *point of the spear* has got along as far as the *middle of the barley-corn,* you should take your barley and *dry it.* How easy would every family, and especially every farmer, do

this, if it were not for the punishment attached to it! The persons, in the "unkent places" before mentioned, dry the malt in their *oven!* But, let us hope, that the labourer will soon be able to get malt without exposing himself to punishment as a *violator of the law.*

KEEPING COWS.

111. As to the *use* of *milk* and of that which proceeds from milk, in a family, very little need be said. At a certain age bread and milk are *all* that a child wants. At a later age they furnish one meal a day for children. Milk is, at all seasons, good to *drink*. In the making of puddings, and in the making of *bread* too, how useful is it! Let any one who has eaten none but baker's bread for a good while, taste bread home-baked, mixed with milk instead of with water; and he will find what the difference is. There is this only to be observed, that, in *hot weather*, bread mixed with milk will not *keep so long* as that mixed with water. It will of course turn *sour* sooner.

112. Whether the milk of a cow be to be consumed by a cottage family in the shape of milk, or whether it be to be made to yield butter, skim-milk, and butter-milk, must depend on circumstances. A woman that has no child, or only one, would, perhaps, find it best to make *some butter* at any rate.

Besides, skim-milk and bread (the milk being boiled) is quite strong food enough for any childrens' breakfast, even when they begin to go to work; a fact which I state upon the most ample and satisfactory experience, very seldom having ever had any other sort of breakfast myself till I was more than ten years old, and I was at work in the fields full four years before that. I will here mention that it gave me singular pleasure to see a boy, just turned of *six*, helping his father *reap*, in Sussex, this last summer. He did little, to be sure ; but it was *something*. His father set him into the ridge at a great distance before him ; and, when he came up to the place, he found a *sheaf* cut ; and, those who know what it is to reap, know how pleasant it is to find now and then a sheaf cut ready to their hand. It was no small thing to see a boy fit to be trusted with so dangerous a thing as a reap-hook in his hands, at an age when " young masters" have nursery-maids to cut their victuals for them, and to see that they do not fall out of window, tumble down stairs, or run under carriage-wheels or horses' bellies. Was not this father discharging his duty by this boy much better than he would have been by sending him to a place called a *school?* The boy is in a school here, and an excellent school too; the school of useful labour. I must hear a great deal more than I ever have yet heard, to convince me, that teaching children to *read* tends so much to their happiness, their independence of spirit, their manliness of character, as teaching them to *reap*. The creature that is in *want* must be a *slave;* and to be habituated *to labour cheerfully* is the only means of preventing nineteen-twentieths of mankind from being in want. I have digressed here; but observations of this sort can, in my opinion, never be too often repeated; especially at a time when all sorts of mad projects are on foot for what is falsely called *educating* the people, and when some would do this by a *tax* that would compel the single man to give part of his earnings to teach the married man's children to read and write.

113. Before I quit the *uses* to which milk may be put, let me mention, that, as mere *drink,* it is, unless, perhaps, in case of heavy labour, better, in my opinion, than any beer, however good. I have drinked little else for the last five years, at any time of the day. Skim-milk I mean. If you have not milk enough to wet up your bread with (for a bushel of flour requires about 16 or 18 pints), you make up the quantity with water, of course; or, which is a very good way, with water that has been put, boiling hot, upon *bran,* and then drained off. This takes the goodness out of the bran to be sure; but, *really good bread* is a thing of so much importance, that it always ought to be the very first object in domestic economy.

114. The cases vary so much, that it is impossible to lay down rules for the application of the produce of a cow, which rules shall fit all cases. I content

myself, therefore, with what has already been said on this subject; and shall only make an observation on the *act of milking*, before I come to the chief matter; namely, the *getting of the food for the cow*. A cow should be milked *clean*. Not a drop, if it can be avoided, should be left in the udder. It has been proved, that the half pint that comes out *last* has *twelve times*, I think it is, as much butter in it, as the half pint that comes out *first*. I tried the milk of ten Alderney cows, and, as nearly as I, without being very nice about the matter, could ascertain, I found the difference to be about what I have stated. The udder would seem to be a sort of milk-pan in which the cream is uppermost, and, of course, comes out last, seeing that the out let is at the bottom. But, besides this, if you do not milk clean, the cow will give less and less milk, and will become dry much sooner than she ought. The *cause* of this I do not know, but experience has long established the fact.

115. In providing food for a cow we must look, first, at the *sort of cow;* seeing that a cow of one sort will certainly require more than twice as much food as a cow of another sort. For a cottage, a cow of the smallest sort common in England is, on every account, the best; and such a cow will not require above 70 or·80 pounds of good moist food in the twenty-four hours.

116. Now, how to raise this food on 40 rods of ground is what we want to know. It frequently happens that a labourer has *more* than 40 rods of ground.

It more frequently happens, that he has some *common*, some *lane*, some little out let or other, for a part of the year, at least. In such cases he may make a different disposition of his ground; or may do with less than the 40 rods. I am here, for simplicity's sake, to suppose, that he have 40 rods of clear, unshaded land, besides what his house and sheds stand upon ; and that he have nothing further in the way of means to keep his cow.

117. I suppose the 40 rods to be *clean* and *unshaded;* for, I am to suppose, that when a man thinks of 5 *quarts of milk a day*, on an average, all the year round, he will not suffer his ground to be encumbered by apple trees that give him only the means of treating his children to fits of the belly-ache, or with currant and gooseberry bushes, which, though their fruit do very well to *amuse*, really give nothing worthy of the name of *food*, except to the Blackbirds and Thrushes. The ground is to be *clear* of trees ; and, in the spring we will suppose it to be *clean*. Then dig it up *deeply*, or, which is better, *trench* it, keeping, however, the top *spit* of the soil *at the top*. Lay it in *ridges* in April or May about two feet apart, and made high and sharp. When the weeds appear about three inches high, turn the ridges into the furrows (*never moving the ground but in dry weather*), and bury all the weeds. Do this as often as the weeds get three inches high : and, by the fall, you will have really clean ground, and not poor ground.

118. There is the ground then, ready. About the 26th of August, but *not earlier*, prepare a rod of your ground, and put some *manure* in it (for *some* you must have), and sow one half of it with Early York Cabbage Seed, and the other half with Sugar Loaf Cabbage Seed, both of the *true* sort, in little drills at 8 inches apart, and the seeds thin in the drill. If the plants come up at two inches apart (and they should be thinned if thicker), you will have a plenty. As soon as fairly out of ground, hoe the ground nicely, and pretty deeply, and again in a few days. When the plants have six leaves, which will be very soon, dig up, make fine, and manure another rod or two, and prick out the plants, 4000 of each in rows at eight inches apart and 3 inches in the row. Hoe the ground between them often, and they will grow fast and be *straight* and strong. I suppose that these beds for plants take 4 rods of your ground. Early in November, or, as the weather may serve, a little earlier, or later, lay some manure (of which I shall say more hereafter) between the ridges, in the other 36 rods, and turn the ridges over on this manure, and then transplant your plants on the ridges at 15 inches apart. Here they will stand the winter; and you must see that the slugs do not eat them. If any plants fail, you have plenty in the bed where you pricked them out; for your 36 rods will not require more than 4000 plants. If the winter be very hard, and bad for plants, you cannot *cover* 36 rods; but, you may the *bed* where the rest of your plants are,

A little litter, or straw, or dead grass, or fern, laid along between the rows and the plants, not to cover the leaves, will preserve them completely. When people complain of *all* their plants being " *cut off*," they have, in fact, nothing to *complain* of but their own extreme carelessness. If I had a gardener who complained of *all* his plants being cut off, I should cut him off pretty quickly. If those in the 36 rods fail, or fail in part, fill up their places, later in the winter, by plants from the bed.

119. If you find the ground dry at top during the winter, hoe it, and particularly near the plants, and rout out all slugs and insects. And, when March comes, and the ground *is dry*, hoe deep and well, and earth the plants up close to the lower leaves. As soon as the plants begin *to grow*, dig the ground with a spade clean and well, and let the spade go as near to the plants as you can without actually *displacing the plants*. Give them another digging in a month; and, if weeds come in the mean-while, *hoe*, and let not one live a week. *f* "Oh! what a deal of *work!*" Well! but, it is for *yourself;* and, besides, it is not all to be done in a day; and, we shall by-and-by, see what it is altogether.

120. By the first of June, I speak of the South of England, and there is also some difference in seasons and soils; but, generally speaking, by the first of June you will have *turned-in* cabbages; and soon you will have the Early Yorks *solid*. And, by the first of June you may get your cow, one that is about

to calve, or that has just calved, and at this time
such a cow as you will want will not, thank God,
cost above five pounds.

121. I shall speak of the place to keep her in and
of the manure and litter, by-and-by. At present I
confine myself to her mere food. The 36 rods, if the
cabbages all stood till they got *solid*, would give her
food for 200 days at 80 pounds weight per day,
which is more than she would eat. But, you must
use some at first, that are not solid ; and, then, some
of them will split before you can use them. But,
you will have pigs to help off with them, and to gnaw
the heads of the stumps. Some of the sugar-loaves
may have been planted out in the spring ; and thus
these 36 rods will get you along to some time in
September.

122. Now, mind, in March, and again in April,
sow more *Early Yorks* and get them to be fine stout
plants, as you did those in the fall. Dig up the
ground and manure it, and, as fast as you cut cabbages, plant cabbages ; and in the same manner and
with the same cultivation as before. Your last
planting will be about the middle of August, with
stout plants, and these will serve you into the month
of November.

123. Now we have to provide from *December to
May inclusive ;* and that, too, out of this same piece
of ground. In November there must be, arrived at
perfection, 3000 turnip plants. These, *without the
greens,* must weigh, on an average, 5 pounds, and

this, at 80 pounds a day will keep the cow 187 days; and there are but 182 days in these six months. The greens will have helped out the latest cabbages to carry you through November; and, perhaps, into December. But, for these six months you must *depend* on nothing but the Swedish turnips.

124. And now how are these to be had *upon the same ground that bears* the cabbages? That we are now going to see. When you plant out your cabbages at the out-set, put first a row of Early Yorks, then a row of Sugar-Loaves, and so on throughout the piece. Of course, as you are to use the Early Yorks first you will cut every other row; and the Early Yorks that you are to plant in summer will go into the intervals. By-and-by the Sugar Loaves are cut away, and in their place will come Swedish turnips, you digging and manuring the ground as in the case of the cabbages; and, at last, you will find about 16 rods where you will have found it too late, and *unnecessary* besides, to plant any second crop of cabbages. Here the Swedish Turnips will stand in rows at 2 feet apart (and always a foot apart in the row;) and thus you will have three thousand turnips; and, if these do not weigh 5 pounds each on an average, the fault must be in the *seed* or in the management.

125. The Swedish Turnips are raised in this manner. You will bear in mind the *four rods* of ground, in which you have sowed and pricked out your cabbage plants. The plants that will be left

there will, in April, serve you for *greens,* if you ever
eat any, though bread and bacon are very good
without greens, and rather better than with. At any
rate, the pig, which has strong powers of digestion,
will consume this herbage. In a part of these four
rods you will, in March and April, as before directed, have sown and raised your Early Yorks for the
summer planting. Now, in the *last week of May,*
prepare a quarter of a rod of this ground, and sow
it, precisely as directed for the Cabbage-seed, with
Swedish turnip-seed; and, sow a quarter of a rod
every three days, till you have sowed *two rods.* If
the *fly appear,* cover the rows over in the *day time*
with cabbage leaves, and take the leaves off at
night; hoe well between the plants; and, when they
are safe from the fly, *thin* them to 4 inches apart in
the row. The two rods will give you nearly *five
thousand plants,* which is 2,000 more than you will
want. From this bed you draw your plants to transplant in the ground where the cabbages have stood,
as before directed. You should transplant none
much *before* the middle of July, and not much *later*
than the middle of August. In the 2 rods, whence
you take your turnip plants, you may leave plants
to come to perfection, at 2 feet distances each way;
and this will give you, *over and above,* 840 pounds
weight of turnips. For the other two rods will be
ground enough for you to sow your cabbage plants
in at the end of August, as directed for last year.

126. I should now proceed to speak of the manner

of harvesting, preserving, and using the crops; of the manner of feeding the cow; of the shed for her; of the managing of the manure, and several other less important things; but, these, for want of room here, must be reserved for the beginning of my next Number. After, therefore, observing, that the Turnip plants must be transplanted in the same way that Cabbage plants are; and that both ought to be transplanted in *dry* weather and in ground just *fresh digged*, I shall close this Number with the notice of two points which I am most anxious to impress upon the mind of every reader.

127. The first is, whether these crops give an *ill taste* to milk and butter. It is very certain, that the taste and smell of certain sorts of cattle-food will do this; for, in some parts of America, where the wild *garlick*, of which the cows are very fond, and which, like other bulbous rooted plants, springs before the grass, not only the milk and butter have a strong taste of garlick, but even the *veal*, when the calves suck milk from such sources. None can be more common expressions, than, in Philadelphia market, are those of *Garlicky Butter* and *Garlicky Veal*. I have distinctly tasted the *Whiskey* in milk of cows fed on distiller's wash. It is also certain, that, if the cow eat *putrid* leaves of cabbages and turnips, the butter will be offensive. And the white-turnip, which is, at best but a poor thing and often half putrid, makes miserable butter. The large *cattle-cabbage*, which, when loaved hard, has a strong

and even an offensive smell, will give a bad taste and smell to milk and butter, whether there be putrid leaves or not. If you boil one of these rank cabbages the water is extremely offensive to the smell. But, I state upon positive and recent experience, that Early York and Sugar-loaf Cabbages will yield as sweet milk and butter *as any food that can be given to a cow*. During this last summer I have, with the exception about to be noticed, kept, from the 1st of May to 22d October, *five cows* upon the grass of *two acres and a quarter of ground, the grass* being generally *cut up for them* and given to them in the stall. I had in the spring 5,000 cabbage plants, intended for my pigs, eleven in number. But, the pigs could not eat *half* their allowance, though they were not very small when they began upon it. We were compelled to resort to the aid of the cows; and, in order to see *the effect on the milk and butter*, we did not *mix* the food; but gave the cows two *distinct spells* at the cabbages, each spell about 10 *days in duration*. The cabbages were cut off the stump with little or no care about *dead leaves*. And sweeter, finer butter, butter of a finer colour, than these cabbages made, never was made in this world. I never had better from cows feeding in the sweetest pasture. Now, as to *Swedish turnips*, they do give a little taste, especially if boiling of the milk pans be neglected, and if the greatest care be not taken about *all* the dairy tackle. Yet, we have, for months together, had the butter so fine from Swedish turnips, that nobody could well distinguish it from grass-butter. But, to secure this, there must be no *sluttishness*. Churn, pans, pail, shelves, wall, floor, and all about the dairy must be clean; and, above all things, the pans must be *boiled*. However, after all, it is not here a case of delicacy of smell so refined as to faint at any thing that meets it except the stink of perfumes. If the butter do taste a little of the Swedish turnip, it will do very well where there is plenty of that sweet sauce which early rising and bodily labour are ever sure to bring.

128. The *other point* (about which I am still more anxious) is, the *seed;* for, if the seed be not *sound* and especially if it be not *true to its kind,* all your labour *is in vain.* It is best, if you can do it, to get your seed from some friend, or some one that you know and can trust. If you save seed, observe all the precautions mentioned in my book on *Gardening.* This very year I have some Swedish turnips, *so called,* about 7,000 in number, and should, if my seed had been *true,* have had about *twenty tons* weight; instead of which I have about *three!* Indeed they are *not Swedish turnips,* but a sort of mixture between that plant and *rape.* I am sure the seedsman did not wilfully deceive me. He was deceived himself. The truth is, that seedsmen are compelled to *buy* their seeds of this plant. *Farmers* save it; and, they but too often pay very little attention to the manner of doing it. The best way is to get a

dozen of fine turnip plants, perfect in all respects, and plant them in a situation where the smell of the blossoms of nothing of the cabbage or rape or turnip or even *charlock* kind can reach them. The seed will keep perfectly good for *four years.*

No. V.

KEEPING COWS.

(Continued.)

129. I HAVE now, in the conclusion of this article, to speak of the manner of *harvesting* and *preserving* the Swedes ; of the *place to keep the cow in ;* of the *manure* for the land ; and of the *quantity of labour,* that the cultivation of the land and the harvesting of the crop will require.

130. *Harvesting and preserving the Swedes.* When they are ready to take up, the tops must be cut off, if not cut off before, and also the *roots ;* but, neither tops nor roots should be cut off *very close.* You will have room for ten bushels of the *bulbs* in the house, or shed. Put the rest into ten-bushel heaps. Make the heap *upon* the ground, in a *round form,* and let it rise up to a point. Lay over it a little litter, straw, or dead grass, about three inches thick ; and then earth upon that about six inches thick. Then cut a

thin round *green turf* about eighteen inches over, and put it upon the crown of the heap to prevent the earth from being washed off. Thus these heaps will remain till wanted for use. When given to the cow, it will be best to *wash* the Swedes and cut each into two or three pieces with a spade or some other tool. You can take in ten bushels at a time. If you find them *sprouting* in the Spring, open the remaining heaps, and expose them to the sun and wind; and cover them again slightly with straw or litter of some sort.

131. *As to the place to keep the cow in*, much will depend upon *situation* and circumstances. I am always supposing that the cottage is a real *cottage*, and not a house in a town or village street; though, wherever there is the quarter of an acre of ground, the cow *may* be kept. Let me, however, suppose that which will generally happen; namely, that the cottage stands by the side of a road, or lane, and amongst fields and woods, if not on the side of a common. To pretend to tell a country labourer how to build a shed for a cow, how to stick it up against the end of his house, or to make it an independent erection; or, to dwell on the materials, where poles, rods, wattles, rushes, furze, heath, and cooper-chips are all to be gotten by him for nothing or next to nothing, would be useless; because a man, who, thus situated, can be at any loss for a shed for his cow, is not only unfit to keep a cow, but unfit to keep a cat. The warmer the shed is the better it is. The floor

F

should *slope*, but not too much. There are *stones*, of some sort or other, every where, and about six wheel-barrow-fulls will *pave* the shed, a thing to be by no means neglected. A broad trough, or box, fixed up at the head of the cow, is the thing to give her food in; and she should be fed three times a day, at least; always at *day-light* and at *sun-set*. It is not *absolutely necessary* that a cow ever quit her shed, except just at calving time, or when taken to the bull. In the former case the time is, nine times out of ten, known to within forty-eight hours. Any enclosed field or place, will do for her during a day or two; and, for such purpose, if there be not room at home, no man will refuse place for her in a fallow field. It will, however, be good, where there is no *common* to turn her out upon, to have her led by a string, two or three times a week, which may be done by a child five years old, to graze, or pick, along the sides of roads and lanes. Where there is a *common*, she will, of course, be turned out in the day time, except in very wet or severe weather; and, in a case like this, a smaller quantity of ground will suffice for the keeping of her. According to the present practice, a miserable "*tallet*" of bad hay is, in such cases, the winter provision for the cow. It can scarcely be called food; and, the consequence is, the cow is both *dry* and *lousy* nearly half the year; instead of being dry only about fifteen days before calving, and being sleek and lusty at the end of the winter, to which a *warm lodging* greatly contributes. For, observe, if you keep a cow, any time between September and June, out in a field, or yard, to endure the chances of the weather, she will not, though she have food precisely the same in quantity and quality, yield above *two-thirds* as much as if she were lodged in house; and in *wet* weather, she will not yield *half* so much. It is not so much the *cold* as the *wet* that is injurious to all our stock in England.

132. *The Manure.* At the *beginning* this must be provided by collections made on the road; by the results of the residence in a cottage. Let any man clean out *every place* about his dwelling; rake and scrape and sweep all into a heap; and he will find, that he has a *great deal.* Earth of almost any sort that has long lain on the surface and has been trodden on is a species of manure. Every act that tends to neatness round a dwelling tends to the creating of a mass of manure. And, I have very seldom seen a cottage, with a plat of ground of a quarter of an acre belonging to it, round about which I could not have collected a very large heap of manure. Every thing of animal or vegetable substance, that comes into a house, must *go out of it again,* in one shape or another. The very emptying of vessels, of various kinds, on a heap of common earth, makes it a heap of the best of manure. Thus goes on the work of *reproduction;* and thus is verified the words of the Scripture: "*Flesh is grass;* and there is *nothing*

F 2

new under the sun." Thus far as to the *out-set.*
When you have *got the cow,* there is no more care
about manure; for, and especially if you have a *pig*
also, you must have enough annually for *an acre* of
ground. And, let it be observed, that, after a time,
it will be unnecessary, and would be injurious, to
manure *for every crop;* for that would produce more
stalk and green than substantial part; as it is well
known, that wheat plants, standing in ground too full
of manure, will yield very thick and long *straws,* but
grains of little or no substance. You ought to depend
more on the spade and the hoe than on the dung-
heap. Nevertheless, the greatest care should be
taken to preserve the manure; because you will
want *straw,* unless you be by the side of a common
which gives you rushes, grassy furze, or fern; and
to get straw you must give a part of your dung from
the cow-stall and pig-stye. The best way to preserve manure, is to have a pit of sufficient dimensions close behind the cow-shed and pig-stye, for
the run from these to go into, and from which all
runs of *rain-water* should be kept. Into this pit
would go the emptying of the shed and of the stye,
and the produce of all sweepings and cleanings
round the house; and thus a large mass of manure
would soon grow together. Much too large a
quantity for a quarter of an acre of ground. One
good load of wheat or rye straw is all that you would
want for the winter, and half a one for the summer;
and you would have more than enough dung to
exchange against this straw.

133. Now, as to *the quantity of labour* that the cultivation of the land will demand *in a year.* We will suppose the whole to have *five complete diggings,* and say nothing about the little matters of sowing and planting and hoeing and harvesting, all which are a mere trifle. We are supposing the owner to be *an able labouring man;* and such a man will dig 12 rod of ground in a day. Here are 200 rods to be digged, and here are a little less than 17 days of work at 12 hours in the day; or, 200 *hours* work, to be done in the course of the long days of spring and summer, while it is light long before *six* in the morning and long after six at night. What *is it,* then! Is it not better than time spent in the ale-house, or in creeping about after a miserable hare? Frequently, and most frequently, there will be a *boy,* if not two, big enough to help. And (I only give this as *a hint*) I saw, on the 7th of November last (1822) a *very pretty woman,* in the village of *Hannington in Wiltshire, digging* a piece of ground and planting it with Early Cabbages, which she did as handily and as neatly as any gardener that I ever saw. The ground was *wet,* and, therefore, *to avoid treading the digged ground in that state,* she had her line extended, and put in the rows as she advanced with her digging, standing *in the trench* while she performed the act of planting, which she did with great nimbleness and precision. Nothing could be more skilfully or beautifully done. Her clothes were neat, clean, and tight about her.

She had turned her handkerchief down from her neck, which, with the glow that the work had brought into her cheeks, formed an object which I do not say would have made me *actually stop my chaise,* had it not been for the occupation in which she was engaged; but, all taken together, the temptation was too strong to be resisted. But, there is the *Sunday;* and I know of no law human or divine, that forbids a labouring man to dig or plant his garden on Sunday, if the good of his family demand it; and if he cannot, without injury to that family, find other time to do it in. Shepherds, carters, pigfeeders, drovers, coachmen, cooks, footmen, printers, and numerous others, work on the Sundays. Theirs are deemed by the law, *works of necessity.* Harvesting and haymaking are allowed to be carried on on the Sunday, in certain cases; when they always are carried on by *provident farmers.* And, I should be glad to know the case which is more a *case of necessity,* than that now under our view. In fact, the labouring people *do work on the Sunday* morning in particular, all over the country, at something or other, or they are engaged in pursuits a good deal less religious than that of digging and planting. So that, as to *the* 200 *hours,* they are easily found, without the loss of any of the time required for constant daily labour.

134. And, what a *produce* is that of a cow! I suppose only an average of 5 *quarts of milk a day.* If made into butter, it will be *equal every week to*

2 *days of the man's wages*, besides the value of the skim milk : and this can hardly be of less value than another day's wages. What a thing, then, is this cow, if she earn half as much as the man! I am greatly under-rating her produce ; but I wish to put all the advantages at the lowest. To be sure, there is work for the wife, or daughters, to milk and make butter. But, the former is done at the two ends of the day, and the latter only about once in the week. And, whatever these may subtract from the *labours of the field*, which all country women ought to be engaged in whenever they conveniently can ; whatever the cares created by the cow may subtract from these is amply compensated for by the *education* that these cares will give to the children. They will *all* learn to milk,* and the girls to make butter. And, which is a thing of the very first importance, they will all learn, from their infancy, to *set a just value upon dumb animals*, and will grow up in the *habit* of treating them with gentleness and feeding them with care. To those who have not been

---

* To me the following has happened within the last year. A young man, in the country, had agreed to be my servant; but, it was found *that he could not milk;* and the bargain was set aside. About a month afterwards, a young man, who said he was a *farmer's son*, and who came from Herefordshire, offered himself to me at Kensington. "Can you *milk ?*" He could not ; but *would learn !* Aye, but, in the learning, he might *dry up my cows !* What a shame to the *parents* of these young men! Both of them were in *want of employment.* The latter had come more than a hundred miles in *search of work ;* and here he was left to hunger still, and to be exposed to all sorts of ills, because he *could not milk.*

brought up in the midst of rural affairs, it is hardly possible to give an adequate idea of the importance of this part of *education*. I should be very loath to entrust the care of my horses, cattle, sheep or pigs, to any one, whose father never had cow or pig of his *own*. It is a general complaint that servants, and especially farm-servants, are not *so good as they used to be*. How should they? They were formerly the sons and daughters of *small farmers;* they are now the progeny of miserable property-less labourers. They have never seen an animal in which they had any interest. They are careless by habit. This monstrous evil has arisen from causes which I have a thousand times described; and which causes must now be speedily removed; or, they will produce a dissolution of society, and give us a *beginning afresh.*

135. The circumstances vary so much, that it is impossible to lay down precise rules suited to all cases. The cottage may be on the side of a forest or common; it may be on the side of a lane or of a great road distant from town or village; it may be on the skirts of one of these latter: and, then, again, the family may be few or great in number, the children small or big: according to all which circumstances the extent and application of the cow-food, and also the application of the produce, will naturally be regulated. Under some circumstances half the above crop may be enough; especially where good commons are at hand. Sometimes it may be

the best way to sell the calf as soon as calved; at others, to fat it; and, at others, if you cannot sell it, which sometimes happens, to knock it on the head as soon as calved; for, where there is a family of small children, the price of a calf at 2 months old cannot be equal to the half of the value of the two months' milk. It is pure weakness to call it "*a pity.*" It is a much greater pity to see hungry children crying for the milk that a calf is sucking to no useful purpose; and as to the cow and the calf, the one must lose her young and the other its life after all, and the respite only makes an addition to the sufferings of both.

136. As to the pretended *unwholesomeness* of milk in certain cases; as to its not being adapted to *some constitutions,* I do not believe one word of the matter. When we talk of the *fruits*, indeed, which were formerly the chief food of a great part of mankind, we should recollect, that those fruits grew in countries that had a *sun to ripen* the fruits and to put nutritious matter into them. But, as to *milk*, England yields to no country upon the face of the earth. Neat cattle will touch nothing that is not wholesome in its nature; nothing that is not wholly innoxious. Out of a pail that has ever had grease in it they will not drink a drop, though they be raging with thirst. Their very breath is fragrance. And how, then, is it possible, that unwholesomeness should distil from the udder of a cow! The milk varies, indeed, in its quality and taste according to

F 5

the variations in the nature of the food; but, no food will a cow touch that is any way hostile to health. Feed young puppies upon *milk from the cow,* and they will never die with that ravaging disease called "*the distemper.*" In short, to suppose that milk contains any thing essentially unwholesome is monstrous. When, indeed, the appetite becomes vitiated; when the organs have been long accustomed to food of a more stimulating nature; when it has been resolved to eat ragouts at dinner and drink wine, and to swallow a "devil" and a glass of strong grog at night; then milk for breakfast may be "*heavy*" and disgusting, and the feeder may stand in need of tea or laudanum, which differ only as to degrees of strength. But, and I speak from the most ample experience, milk is not "*heavy,*" and much less is it *unwholesome,* when he who uses it rises early, never swallows strong drink, and never *stuffs* himself with flesh of any kind. Many and many a day I scarcely taste of meat, and then chiefly at *breakfast,* and that, too, at an early hour. Milk is the natural food of *young people:* if it be too rich, *skim* it again and again till it be not too rich. This is an evil easily cured. If you have now to *begin* with a family of children, they may not like it at first. But, *persevere;* and the parent who does not do this, having the means in his hands, shamefully neglects his duty. A son who prefers a "devil" and a glass of grog to a hunch of bread and a bowl of cold milk, I regard as a pest; and for this pest the father has to thank himself.

137. Before I dismiss this article, let me offer an observation or two to those persons, who live in the vicinity of towns, or in towns, and who, though they have *large gardens*, have " *no land to keep a cow*," a circumstance which they " *exceedingly regret.*" I have, I dare say, witnessed this case at least a thousand times. Now, how much garden ground does it require to supply even a large family with *garden vegetables?* The market gardeners round the metropolis of this wen-headed country; round this wen of all wens; round this prodigious and monstrous collection of human beings : these market gardeners have about *three hundred thousand families to supply with vegetables*, and these they supply well too, and with summer-fruits into the bargain. Now, if it demanded *ten rods to a family*, the whole would demand, all but a fraction, *nineteen thousand acres of garden ground.* We have only to cast our eyes over what there is, to know, that there is not a *fourth* of that quantity. A *square mile* contains, leaving out parts of a hundred, 700 acres of land ; and 19,000 acres occupy more than *twenty-two square miles.* Are there 22 square miles covered with the Wen's market gardens ? The very question is absurd. The whole of the market gardens from Brompton to Hammersmith, extending to Battersea Rise on the one side and to the Bayswater road on the other side, and leaving out roads, lanes,

nurseries, pastures, cornfields, and pleasure grounds, do not, in my opinion, cover *one square mile*. To the north and south of the Wen there is very little in the way of market garden ; and if, on both sides of the Thames, to the eastward of the Wen, there be *three square miles* actually covered with market gardens, that is the full extent. How, then, could the Wen be supplied, if it required *ten rods* to each family ? To be sure, potatoes, carrots and turnips, and especially the first of these, are brought, for the use of the Wen, from a great distance, in many cases. But, so they are for the use of the persons I am speaking of ; for a gentleman thinks no more of raising a large quantity of these things in his *garden* than he thinks of *raising wheat there*. How is it, then, that it requires half an acre, or 80 rods, in a *private* garden to supply a family, while these market-gardeners supply all these families (and so amply too) from ten, or more likely, five rods of ground to a family ? I have shown, in the last Number, that nearly fifteen tons of vegetables can be raised in a year upon forty rods of ground ; that is to say, *ten loads* for a *wagon and four good horses*. And is not a fourth, or even an eighth, part of this weight, sufficient to go down the throats of a family in a year ? Nay, allow that only *a ton* goes to a family in a year, it is more than *six pounds weight a day ;* and what sort of family must that be that really *swallows* six pounds weight a day ; and this a market-gardener will raise for them upon less than *three rods* of ground; for he will raise, in the course of the year, even more than fifteen tons upon forty rods of ground. What is it, then, that they *do* with the eighty rods of ground in a private garden ? Why, in the first place, they have *one crop* where they ought to have *three*. Then they do not half *till* the ground. Then they grow things that are *not wanted*. Plant cabbages and other things, let them stand till they be good for nothing, and then wheel them to the rubbish heap. Raise as many radishes, lettuces, and as much endive and as many kidney-beans, as would serve for ten families ; and finally throw nine-tenths of them away. I once saw not less than three rods of ground, in a garden of this sort, with lettuces all bearing *seed*. Seed enough for half a county. They cut cabbage *here* and a cabbage *there*, and so let the whole of the piece of ground remain undug, till the *last* cabbage be cut. But, after all, the produce, even in this way is so great, that it never could be gotten rid of, if the main part were not *thrown away*. The rubbish heap always receives four-fifths even of the *eatable* part of the produce.

138. It is not thus that the market-gardeners proceed. Their rubbish heap consists of little besides mere cabbage-stumps. No sooner is one crop *on* the ground than they settle in their minds what is to follow it. They *clear as they go* in taking off a crop, and, as they clear they dig and plant. The ground is never without seed in it or plants on it. And thus in the course of the year, they raise a prodigious

bulk of vegetables from 80 rods of ground. Such vigilance and industry are not to be expected in a *servant;* for, it is foolish to expect, that a man will exert himself for another as much as he will for himself. But, if I were situated as one of the persons is that I have spoken of in paragraph 137; that is to say, if I had a garden of 80 rods, or even of 60 rods, of ground, I would, out of that garden, draw a sufficiency of vegetables for my family, and would make it yield enough for a *cow* besides. I should go a short way to work with my gardener. I should put *Cottage Economy* into his hands, and tell him, that, if he could furnish me with vegetables and my cow with food, he was my man; and, that, if he could not, I must get one that could and would. I am not for making a man toil like a slave; but, what would become of the world, if a well-fed healthy man could exhaust himself in tilling and cropping and clearing half an acre of ground! I have known many men *dig* 30 rods of garden-ground in a day; I have, before I was fourteen, digged 20 rods in a day for more than ten days successively; and I have heard, and believe the fact, of a man, at Portsea, who digged 40 rods in one single day, between day-light and dark. So that it is no slavish toil that I am here recommending.

139. Next after the *Cow* comes the *Pig*; and, in many cases, where a cow cannot be kept a pig or pigs may be kept. But, these are animals not to be ventured on without due consideration as to the means of *feeding* them; for, a starved pig is a great deal worse than none at all. You cannot make bacon, as you can milk, merely out of the garden. There must be *something more*. A couple of flitches of bacon are worth fifty thousand methodist sermons and religious tracts. The sight of them upon the rack tends more to keep a man from poaching and stealing than whole volumes of penal statutes, though assisted by the terrors of the hulks and the gibbet. They are great softeners of the temper and promoters of domestic harmony. They are a great blessing ; but, they are not to be had from *herbage* or *roots* of any kind ; and, therefore, before a *pig* be attempted, the means ought to be considered.

140. *Breeding sows* are great favourites with Cottagers in general ; but I have seldom known them to answer their purpose. Where there is an outlet, the sow will, indeed, keep herself by grazing in summer, with a little *wash* to help her out ; and, when her pigs come, they are many in number ; but, they are a heavy expense. The sow must live as well as a *fatting hog*, or the pigs will be good for little. It is a great mistake, too, to suppose, that the

condition of the sow *previous to pigging* is of no
consequence; and, indeed, some suppose, that she
ought to be rather *bare of flesh* at the pigging time.
Never was a greater mistake; for, if she be in this
state, she presently becomes a mere rack of bones;
and then, do what you will, the pigs will be poor
things. However fat she may be before she farrow,
the pigs will make her lean in a week. All her fat
goes away in her milk, and, unless the pigs have a
store to draw upon, they pull her down directly; and,
by the time they are three weeks old, they are starv-
ing for want; and then they never come to good.

141. Now, a cottager's sow cannot, without great
expense, be kept in a way to enable her to meet the
demands of her farrow. She may *look* pretty well;
but the flesh she has upon her is not of the same nature as that which the *farm yard* sow carries about
her. It is the result of grass, and of poor grass, too,
or other weak food; and not made partly out of corn
and whey and strong wash, as in the case of the farmer's sow. No food short of that of a fatting hog
will enable her to keep her pigs *alive;* and, this she
must have for *ten weeks*, and that at a great expense.
Then comes the operation, upon the principle of
Parson Malthus, in order to *check population;* and
there is some risk here, though not very great. But,
there is the *weaning;* and who, that knows any thing
about the matter, will think lightly of the weaning of
a farrow of pigs! By having nice food given them,
they seem, for a few days, not to miss their mother

But, their appearance soon shews the want of her.
Nothing but the very best food, and that given in the
most judicious manner, will keep them up to any
thing like good condition; and, indeed, there is nothing short of *milk* that will effect the thing well.
How should it be otherwise? The very richest cow's
milk is poor, compared with that of the sow; and, to
be taken from this and put upon food one ingredient
of which is *water*, is quite sufficient to reduce the
poor little things to bare bones and staring hair, a
state to which a cottager's pigs very soon come in
general; and, at last, he frequently drives them to
market, and sells them for less than the cost of the
food which they and the sow have devoured since
they were farrowed. It was, doubtless, pigs of this
description that were sold the other day at Newbury
Market, for *fifteen pence apiece*, and which were, I
dare say, dear even as a gift. To get such a pig to
begin to grow will require *three months*, and with
good feeding too, in winter time. To be sure it does
come to be a hog at last; but, do what you can, it is
a dear hog.

142. The *Cottager*, then, can hold no competition
with the *Farmer* in the *breeding* of pigs, to do which,
with advantage, there must be *milk*, and milk, too,
that can be advantageously applied to no other use.
The cottager's pig must be bought ready weaned to
his hand, and, indeed, at *four months old*, at which
age, if he be in good condition, he will eat any thing
that an old hog will eat. He will graze, eat cabbage

eaves and almost the stumps, Swedish turnip tops
or roots; and such things, with a little wash, will
keep him along in very good growing order. I have
now to speak of the time of purchasing, the manner
of keeping, of fatting, killing and curing; but these
I must reserve till my next Number.

No. VI.

KEEPING PIGS.

(Continued.)

143. As in the case of cows so in that of pigs,
much must depend upon the situation of the cottage;
because all pigs will *graze;* and, therefore, on the
skirts of forests or commons, a couple or three pigs
may be kept, if the family be considerable; and
especially if the cottager brew his own beer, which
will give him grains to assist the wash. Even in
lanes, or on the sides of great roads, a pig will find a
good part of his food from May to November; and,
if he be *yoked,* the occupiers of the neighbourhood
must be churlish and brutish indeed, if they give the
owner any annoyance.

144. Let me break off here for a moment to point
out to my readers the truly excellent conduct of Lord
Winchelsea and Lord Stanhope, who, as I read,

have taken great pains to make the labourers on their estates comfortable by allotting to each a piece of ground sufficient for the keeping of a cow. I once, when I lived at Botley, proposed to the copy-holders and other farmers in my neighbourhood, that we should petition the Bishop of Winchester, who was lord of the manors thereabouts, to grant titles to all the numerous persons called *trespassers on the wastes;* and also to give titles to others of the poor parishioners, who were willing to make, on the skirts of the wastes, enclosures not exceeding an acre each. This, I am convinced, would have done a great deal towards relieving the parishes, then greatly burdened by men out of work. This would have been better than digging holes one day to fill them up the next. Not a single man would agree to my proposal! One, a bull-frog farmer (now, I hear, pretty well sweated down), said it would only make them *saucy!* And one, a true disciple of *Malthus,* said, that to facilitate their rearing of children *was a harm!* This man had, at the time, in his own occupation, land that had formerly been *six farms,* and he had, too, ten or a dozen children. I will not mention names ; but, this farmer will *now,* perhaps, have occasion to call to mind what I told him on that day, when his opposition, and particularly the ground of it, gave me the more pain as he was a very industrious, civil and honest man. Never was there a greater mistake than to suppose, that men are made saucy and idle by just and kind treatment. *Slaves* are always lazy and saucy : nothing but the lash will extort from them either labour or respectful deportment. I never met with a *saucy* Yankee (New Englander) in my life. Never servile; always civil. This must necessarily be the character of *freemen living in a state of competence.* They have nobody to envy ; nobody to complain of; they are in good humour with mankind. It must, however, be confessed, that very little, comparatively speaking, is to be accomplished by the individual efforts, even of benevolent men like the two noblemen before mentioned. They have a strife to maintain against the *general tendency of the national state of things.* It is by general and indirect means, and not by partial and direct and positive regulations, that so great a good as that which they generously aim at can be accomplished. When we are to see such means adopted, God only knows; but, if much longer delayed, I am of opinion, that they will come too late to prevent something very much resembling a dissolution of society.

145. The cottager's pig should be bought in the spring, or late in winter ; and, being then four months old, he will be a year old before killing time ; for, it should always be borne in mind, that this age is required in order to insure the greatest quantity of meat from a given quantity of food. If a hog be more than a year old, he is the better for it. The flesh is more solid and more nutritious than that of a young hog, much in the same degree that the mutton of a full-mouthed wether is better than that of a

younger wether. The pork or bacon of young hogs, even if fatted on corn, is very apt to *boil out*, as they call it; that is to say, come out of the pot smaller in bulk than it goes in. When you begin to fat, do it by degrees, especially in the case of hogs under a year old. If you feed *high* all at once, the hog is apt to *surfeit*, and then a great loss of food takes place. Peas, or barley-meal is the food; the latter rather the best, and does the work quicker. Make him *quite fat* by all means. The last bushel, even if he sit as he eat, is the most profitable. If he can walk two hundred yards at a time, he is not well-fatted. Lean bacon is the most wasteful thing that any family can use. In short, it is uneatable, except by drunkards, who want something to stimulate their sickly appetite. The man who cannot live on *solid fat* bacon, well fed and well cured, wants the sweet sauce of labour, or is fit for the hospital. But, then, it must be *bacon*, the effect of barley or peas (not beans), and not of whey, potatoes, or *messes* of any kind. It is frequently said, and I know that even farmers say it, that bacon, made from corn, *costs more than it is worth!* Why do they take care to have it, then? They know better. They know well, that it is the very *cheapest* they can have; and they, who look at both ends and both sides of every cost, would as soon think of shooting their hogs as of fatting them on *messes;* that is to say, for *their own use*, however willing they might now-and-then be to regale the Londoners with a bit of potatoe-pork.

146. About *Christmas*, if the weather be coldish, is a good time to kill. If the weather be very mild, you may wait a little longer; for the hog cannot be too fat. The day before killing, he should have no food. To kill a hog nicely is so much of a profession, that it is better to pay a shilling for having it done, than to stab and hack and tear the carcass about. I shall not speak of *pork;* for I would by no means recommend it. There are two ways of going to work to make bacon; in the one you take off the hair by *scalding*. This is the practice in most parts of England and all over America. But, the *Hampshire* way, and best way, is to *burn the hair off*. There is a great deal of difference in the consequences. The first method slackens the skin, opens all the pores of it, makes it loose and flabby by drawing out the roots of the hair. The second tightens the skin in every part, contracts all the sinews and vieus in the skin, makes the flitch a solider thing, and the skin a better protection to the meat. The taste of the meat is very different from that of a scalded hog; and to this chiefly it was that Hampshire bacon owed its reputation for excellence. As the hair is to be *burnt* off, it must be *dry*, and care must be taken, that the hog be kept on dry litter of some sort the day previous to killing. When killed he is laid upon a narrow bed of straw, not wider than his carcass, and only two or three inches thick. He is then covered all over thinly with straw, to which, according as the wind may be, the fire is put at one end. As the straw

burns, it burns the hair. It requires two or three coverings and burnings, and care is taken, that the skin be not, in any part burnt, or parched. When the hair is all burnt off close, the hog is *scraped* clean, but never touched with *water*. The upper side being finished, the hog is turned over, and the other side is treated in like manner. This work should always be done *before day-light ;* for, in the day-light, you cannot so nicely discover whether the hair be sufficiently burnt off. The light of the fire is weakened by that of the day. Besides, it makes the boys get up very early for once at any rate, and that is something ; for boys always like a bonfire.

147. The *inwards* are next taken out, and if the wife be not a slattern, here, in the mere offal, in the mere garbage, there is food, and delicate food too, for a large family for a week ; and hogs'-puddings for the children, and some for neighbours' children who come to play with them ; for these things are by no means to be overlooked, seeing that they tend to the keeping alive of that affection in children for their parents, which, later in life, will be found absolutely necessary to give effect to wholesome precept, especially when opposed to the boisterous passions of youth.

148. The butcher, the next day, cuts the hog up ; and then the house is *filled with meat !* Souse, griskins, blade-bones, thigh-bones, spare-ribs, chines, belly-pieces, cheeks, all coming into use one after the other, and the last of the latter not before the end

of about four or five weeks. But, about this time, it is more than possible, that the Methodist parson will pay you a visit. It is remarked in America, that these gentry are attracted by the squeaking of the pigs as the fox is by the cackling of the hen. This may be slander; but, I will tell you what I did know to happen. A good honest, careful fellow had a spare-rib, on which he intended to sup with his family after a long and hard day's work at coppice-cutting. Home he came at dark with his two little boys, each with a nitch of wood that they had carried four miles, cheered with the thought of the repast that awaited them. In he went, found his wife, the Methodist parson and a whole troop of the sisterhood, engaged in prayer, and on the table lay scattered the clean-polished bones of the spare-rib! Can any reasonable creature believe, that, to save the soul, God requires us to give up the food necessary to sustain the body? Did Saint Paul preach this? He, who, while he spread the Gospel abroad, *worked himself*, in order to have to give to those who were unable to work? Upon what, then, do these modern Saints, these Evangelical gentlemen, found their claim to live on the labour of others?

149. All the other parts taken away, the two sides that remain, and that are called *flitches,* are to be cured for *bacon.* They are first rubbed with salt on their insides, or flesh sides, then placed, one on the other, the flesh sides uppermost, in a salting-trough, which has a gutter round its edges to drain away the

brine; for, to have sweet and fine bacon, the flitches must not lie sopping in brine, which gives it that sort of taste which barrel-pork and sea-jonck have, and than which nothing is more villainous. Every one knows how different is the taste of fresh dry salt, from that of salt in a dissolved state. The one is savoury, the other nauseous. Therefore, *change the salt often.* Once in four or five days. Let it melt, and sink in; but, let it not lie too long. Change the flitches. Put that at bottom which was first put on the top. Do this a couple of times. This mode will cost you a great deal more in salt, or rather in *taxes,* than the *sopping* mode; but, without it, your bacon will not be sweet and fine, and *will not keep so well.* As to the *time* required for making the flitches sufficiently salt, it depends on circumstances; the thickness of the flitch, the state of the weather, the place wherein the salting is going on. It takes a longer time for a thick than for a thin flitch; it takes longer in dry than in damp weather; it takes longer in a dry than in a damp place. But, for the flitches of a hog of twelve score, in weather not very dry or very damp, about six weeks may do; and, as yours is to be *fat,* which receives little injury from over-salting, give time enough; for you are to have bacon till Christmas comes again. The place for salting should, like a dairy, always be cool, but always admit a *free circulation of air: confined* air, though *cool,* will taint meat sooner than the midday sun accompanied with a breeze. Ice will

G

not melt in the hottest sun so soon as in a close and damp cellar. Put a lump of ice in *cold water*, and one of the same size before a *hot fire*, and the former will dissolve in half the time that the latter will. Let me take this occasion of observing, that an ice-house should never be *under ground*, nor *under the shade of trees*. That the bed of it ought to be three feet above the level of the ground; that this bed ought to consist of something that will admit the drippings to go instantly off; and that the house should stand in a place *open to the sun and air*. This is the way that they have ice-houses under the burning sun of Virginia; and here they keep their fish and meat as fresh and sweet as in winter, when at the same time, neither will keep for twelve hours, though let down to the depth of a hundred feet in a well. A Virginian, with some poles and straw, will stick up an ice-house for ten dollars, worth a dozen of those ice-houses, each of which costs our men of taste as many scores of pounds. It is very hard to imagine, indeed, what any one should want ice *for*, in a country like this, except for clodpole boys to slide upon and to drown cockneys in skating-time; but, if people must have ice in summer, they may as well go a right way as a wrong way to get it.

150. However, the patient that I have at this time, under my hands, wants nothing to cool his blood, but something to warm it, and, therefore, I will get back to the flitches of bacon, which are now to be *smoked;* for, smoking is a great deal better than

merely *drying*, as is the fashion in the dairy-countries in the West of England. When there were plenty of *farm*-houses, there were plenty of places to smoke bacon in; since farmers have lived in gentlemen's houses and the main part of the farm-houses have been knocked down, these places are not so plenty. However, there is scarcely any neighbourhood without a chimney left to hang bacon up in. Two precautions are necessary: first to hang the flitches where no *rain* comes down upon them : second, not to let them be so near the fire as to *melt*. These precautions taken, the next is, that the smoke must proceed from *wood*, not turf, peat, or coal. Stubble, or litter might do; but the trouble would be great. *Fir*, or *deal*, smoke is not fit for the purpose. I take it, that the absence of wood, as fuel, in the dairy countries, and in the North, has led to the making of pork and dried bacon. As to the *time* that it requires to smoke a flitch, it must depend a good deal upon whether there be a *constant fire* beneath, and whether the fire be large or small. A month may do, if the fire be pretty constant and such as a farm-house fire usually is. . But, over-smoking, or rather, too long hanging in the air, makes the bacon *rust*. Great attention should, therefore, be paid to this matter. The flitch ought not to be dried up to the hardness of a board, and yet it ought to be perfectly dry. Before you hang it up, lay it on the floor, scatter the flesh-side pretty thickly over with bran, or with some fine saw-dust other than

G 2

that of deal or fir. Rub it on the flesh, or pat it well down upon it. This keeps the smoke from getting into the little openings, and makes a sort of crust to be dried on ; and, in short, keeps the flesh cleaner than it would otherwise be.

151. To keep the bacon sweet and good, and free from nasty things that they call *hoppers;* that is to say, a sort of skipping maggots, engendered by a fly which has a great relish for bacon : to provide against this mischief, and also to keep the bacon from becoming rusty, the Americans, whose country is so hot in summer, have two methods. They smoke no part of the hog except the hams, or gammons. They cover these with coarse linen cloth, such as the finest hop-bags are made of, which they sew neatly on. They then *white-wash* the cloth all over with *lime* white-wash, such as we put on walls, their lime being excellent stone-lime. They give the ham four or five washings, the one succeeding as the former gets dry ; and, in the sun, all these washings are put on in a few hours. The flies cannot get through this ; and thus the meat is preserved from them. The *other* mode, and that is the mode for you, is, to sift *fine* some clean and dry *wood-ashes.* Put some at the bottom of a box, or chest, which is long enough to hold a flitch of bacon. Lay in one flitch. Then put in more ashes. Then the *other flitch;* and then cover this with six or eight inches of the ashes. This will effectually keep away all flies ; and will keep the bacon as fresh and good as when it

came out of the chimney, which it will not be for any great length of time, if put on a rack, or kept hung up in the open air. *Dust*, or even *sand*, very, very *dry*, would, perhaps, do as well. The object is not only to keep out the flies but the *air*. The place where the chest, or box, is kept, ought to be *dry;* and, if the ashes should get damp (as they are apt to do from the salts they contain) they should be put in the fire-place to dry, and then be put back again. Peat-ashes, or turf-ashes, might do very well for this purpose. With these precautions, the bacon will be as good at the end of the year as on the first day; and it will keep two and even three years perfectly good, for which, however, there can be no necessity.

152. Now, then, this hog is altogether a capital thing. The other parts will be meat for about four or five weeks. The *lard*, nicely put down, will last a long while for all the purposes for which it is wanted. To make it keep well there should be some salt put into it. Country-children are badly brought up, if they do not like sweet lard spread upon bread, as we spread butter. Many a score hunchs of this sort have I eaten, and I never knew what poverty was. I have eaten it for luncheon at the houses of good substantial farmers in France and Flanders. I am not now frequently so hungry as I ought to be; but, I should think it no hardship to eat *sweet* lard instead of butter. But, now-a-days, the labourers, and especially the female part of them, have fallen into

the taste of *niceness* in food and *finery in dress* ; a
quarter of a belly full and rags are the consequence.
The food of their choice is high-priced, so that, for
the greater part of their time, they are half-starved.
The dress of their choice is *showy* and *flimsy*, so
that, to-day they are *ladies*, and to-morrow ragged as
sheep with the scab. But, has not nature made the
country girls as pretty as ladies ? Oh, yes ! (bless
their rosy cheeks and white teeth !) and a great deal
prettier too ! But, are they *less* pretty, when their
dress is plain and substantial, and when the natural
presumption is, that they have smocks as well as
gowns, than they are when drawn off in the frail
fabric of Sir Robert Peel, " where taudry colours
strive with dirty white," exciting violent suspicions,
that all is not as it ought to be nearer the skin, and
calling up a train of ideas extremely hostile to that
sort of feeling which every lass innocently and com-
mendably wishes to awaken in her male beholders ?
Are they prettiest when they come through the wet
and dirt safe and neat ; or, when their draggled
dress is plastered to their backs by a shower of
rain ? However, the fault has not been theirs nor
that of their parents. It is *the system* of managing
the affairs of the nation. This system has made all
flashy and *false*, and has put all things out of their
place. Pomposity, bombast, hyperbole, redundancy,
and obscurity both in speaking and in writing ; mock-
delicacy in manners ; mock-liberality, mock-hu-
manity, and, mock-religion Pitt's false money,

Peel's flimsy dresses, Wilberforce's potatoe diet, Castlereagh and Mackintosh's oratory, Walter Scott's poems, Walter's and Stoddart's paragraphs, with all the bad taste and baseness and hypocrisy which they spread over this country; all have arisen, grown, branched out, bloomed and borne together; and we are now beginning to taste of their fruit. But, as the fat of the adder is, as is said, the antidote to its sting; so in the Son of the great worker of Spinning-Jennies, we have, thanks to the Proctors and Doctors of Oxford, the author of that *Bill*, before which this false, this flashy, this flimsy, this rotten system will dissolve as one of his father's pasted calicoes does at the sight of the washing-tub.

153. "What," says the Cottager, "has all this to do with hogs and bacon?" Not directly with hogs and bacon, indeed; but, it has a great deal to do, my good fellow, with your affairs, as I shall, probably, hereafter more fully show, though I shall now leave you to the enjoyment of your flitches of bacon, which, as I before observed, will do ten thousand times more than any Methodist parson, or any other parson (except, of course, those of *our* church) to make you happy, not only in this world, but in the world to come. *Meat in the House* is a great source of *harmony*, a great preventer of the temptation to commit those things, which, from small beginnings, lead, finally, to the most fatal and atrocious results; and, I hold that doctrine to be *truly damnable*, which teaches, that God has made any selection, any con-

dition relative to belief, which is to save from punishment those who violate the principles of *natural justice.*

154. *Some* other meat you may have; but, bacon is the great thing. It is always ready; as good cold as hot; goes to the field or the coppice conveniently; in harvest and other busy times demands the pot to be boiled only on a Sunday; has twice as much strength in it as any other thing of the same weight; and, in short, has in it every quality that tends to make a labourer's family able to work and well off. One pound of bacon, such as that which I have described, is, in a labourer's family, worth four or five of ordinary mutton or beef, which are great part *bone*, and which, in short, are gone in a moment. But always observe, it is *fat bacon* that I am talking about There will, in spite of all that can be done, be *some* lean in the gammons, though comparatively very little; and, therefore, you ought to begin at that end of the flitches; for, *old lean bacon* is not good.

155. Now, as to the *cost.* A pig (a *spayed sow* is best) bought in March, four months old, can be had now for fifteen shillings. The cost till fatting time is next to nothing to a Cottager; and then the cost, at the present price of corn, would, for a hog of twelve score, not exceed *three pounds;* in the whole *four pounds five;* a pot of poison a week bought at the public house comes to *twenty-six shillings* of the money; and more than *three times the remainder* is generally flung away upon the miserable *tea*, as I have

clearly shewn in the First Number, at Paragraph 24. I have, indeed there shown, that, if the tea were laid aside, the labourer might supply his family well with beer all the year round, and have a fat hog of even *fifteen score* for the *cost of the tea*, which does him and can do him *no good at all*.

156. The feet, the cheeks, and other bone being considered, the *bacon and lard*, taken together, would not exceed *sixpence a pound*. Irish bacon is " *cheaper*." Yes, *lower priced*. But, I will engage, that a pound of mine, when it comes *out* of the pot (to say nothing of the *taste*), shall weigh as much as a *pound and a half* of Irish, or any dairy or slop-fed bacon, when that comes out of the pot. No, no : the farmers joke, when they say, that their bacon *costs them more than* they could buy bacon for. They know well what it is they are doing; and besides, they always forget, or, rather, remember not to say, that the fatting of a large hog yields them three or four load of dung, really worth more than ten or fifteen of common yard dung. In short, without hogs, farming *could not go on ;* and it never has gone on in any country in the world. The hogs are the great *stay* of the whole concern. They are *much in small space ;* they make no *show*, as flocks and herds do ; but, without them, the cultivation of the land would be a poor, a miserably barren concern.

157. *Very fat* Mutton may be salted to great advantage, and also smoked, and may be kept thus a long while. Not the shoulders and legs, but the *back* of the sheep. I have never made any flitch of *sheep-bacon;* but, I will; for, there is nothing like having a *store* of meat in a house. The running to the butcher's daily is a ridiculous thing. The very idea of being fed, of *a family* being fed, by daily supplies, has something in it perfectly *tormenting*. One-half of the time of a mistress of a house, the affairs of which are carried on in this way, is taken up in talking about what is to be got for dinner, and in negociations with the butcher. One single moment spent at table beyond what is absolutely necessary is a moment very shamefully spent; but, to suffer a system of domestic economy, which unnecessarily wastes daily an hour or two of the mistress's time in hunting for the provision for the repast, is a shame indeed; and, when we consider, how much time is generally spent in this and in equally absurd ways, it is no wonder, that we see so little performed by numerous individuals as they do perform during the course of their lives.

158 *Very fat parts of Beef* may be salted and smoked in a like manner. Not the *lean;* for that is a great waste, and is, in short, good for nothing. Poor fellows on board of ships are compelled to eat it; but, it is a very bad thing.

BEES, FOWLS, &c. &c.

159. I NOW proceed to treat of objects of less importance than the foregoing, but still such as may be worthy of great attention. If all of them cannot be expected to come within the scope of the care of a labourer's family, some of them must, and others may: and, it is always of great consequence, that children be brought up to set a just value upon all useful things, and especially upon all *living things;* to know the *utility* of them : for, without this, they never, when grown up, are worthy of being entrusted with the *care* of them. One of the greatest, and, perhaps, the very commonest, fault of servants, is, their inadequate care of animals committed to their charge. It is a well-known saying, that " the *master's eye* makes the horse fat ;" and the remissness, to which this alludes, is generally owing to the servant not having been brought up to feel *an interest* in the well-being of animals.

BEES.

160. It is not my intention to enter into a history of this insect, about which so much has been written, especially by the French naturalists. It is the *useful* that I shall treat of, and that is done in not many words. The best *hives* are those made of clean, unblighted *rye-straw*. Boards are too cold in England. A swarm should always be put into a *new* hive, and the sticks should be *new* that are put into the hive for the bees to work on; for, if the hive be old, it is not so *wholesome*, and a thousand to one but it contain the embryos of *moths* and other insects injurious to bees. Over the hive itself there should be a cap of thatch, made also of clean rye-straw; and it should not only be *new* when first put on the hive; but, a new one should be made to supply the place of the former one every three or four months; for, when the straw begins to get rotten, as it soon does, insects breed in it, its smell is bad, and its effect on the bees is dangerous.

161. The hives should be placed on a bench, the legs of which mice and rats cannot creep up. Tin round the legs is best. But, even this will not keep down *ants*, which are mortal enemies of bees. To keep these away, if you find them infest the hive, take a green stick and twist it round in the shape of a ring, to lay on the ground, round the leg of the bench, and at a few inches from it; and cover this stick with *tar*. This will keep away the ants. If the ants come from one home, you may easily *trace them to it;* and when you have found it, pour *boiling water* on it in the night, when all the family are at home. This is the only effectual way of destroying ants, which are frequently so troublesome. It would be cruel to cause this destruction, if it were not

necessary to do it, in order to preserve the honey, and, indeed, the bees too.

162. Besides the hive and its cap, there should be a sort of shed, with top, back, and ends, to give additional protection in winter; though, in summer, hives may be kept *too hot*, and, in that case, the bees become sickly and the produce becomes light. The *situation* of the hive is to face the South-east; or, at any rate, to be sheltered from the *North* and the *West*. From the North always, and from the West in winter. If it be a very dry season in summer, it contributes greatly to the success of the bees, to place clear water near their home, in a thing that they can conveniently drink out of; for, if they have to go a great way for drink, they have not much time for work.

163. It is supposed, that bees live only a year; at any rate, it is best never to keep the same stall, or family, over two years, except you want to increase your number of hives. The swarm of *this summer* should always be taken in the autumn of next year. It is whimsical to *save* the bees when you take the honey. You must *feed* them; and, if saved, they will die of old age before the next fall; and though young ones will supply the place of the dead, this is nothing like a good swarm put up during the summer

164. As to the things that bees make their collections from, we do not, perhaps, know a thousandth part of them; but of all the blossoms that they seek

eagerly, that of the *Buck-wheat* stands foremost.
Go round a piece of this grain just towards sunset,
when the Buck-wheat is in bloom, and you will see
the air filled with bees, going home from it in all
directions. The Buck-wheat, too, continues in bloom
a long while; for, the grain is dead ripe on one part
of the plant, while there are fresh blossoms coming
out on the other part.

165. A good stall of bees, that is to say, the produce of one, is always worth about *two bushels of
good wheat.* The *cost* is nothing to the labourer.
He must be a stupid countryman indeed, who cannot make a bee-hive; and a lazy one indeed if he
will not, if he can. In short, there is nothing but
care demanded; and there are very few situations in
the country, especially in the south of England,
where a labouring man may not have half a dozen
stalls of bees to take every year. The main things
are to keep away insects, mice, and birds, and especially a little bird, called the bee-bird; and to keep
all clean and fresh as to the hives and coverings.
Never put a swarm into an *old hive.* If wasps, or
hornets, annoy you, watch them home in the day
time; and, in the night kill them by fire, or by boiling water. Fowls should not go where bees are, for
they eat them.

166. Suppose a man get three stalls of bees in
a year. Six bushels of wheat give him bread for an
eighth part of the year. Scarcely any thing is a

greater misfortune than *shiftlessness.* It is an evil
little short of the loss of eyes, or of limbs.

GEESE.

167. They can be kept to advantage only where
there are *green commons,* and there they are easily
kept; live to a very great age; and are amongst the
hardiest animals in the world. If *well kept,* a goose
will lay a hundred eggs in a year. The French put
their eggs under large hens of common fowls, to each
of which they give four or five eggs; or under turkeys, to which they give nine or ten goose-eggs. If
the goose herself sit, she must be well and *regularly
fed,* at, or near to, her nest. When the young ones
are hatched, they should be kept in a warm place
for about four days, and fed on barley-meal, mixed,
if possible, with milk; and then they will begin to
graze. Water for them, or for the old ones, to *swim*
in, is by no means *necessary,* nor, perhaps, ever even
useful. Or, how is it, that you see such fine flocks
of fine geese all over Long Island (in America) where
there is scarcely such a thing as a pond or a run of
water?

168. Geese are raised by *grazing;* but, to *fat*
them something more is required. Corn of some
sort, or boiled swedish turnips. Some corn and some
raw swedish turnips, or carrots, or white cabbages or
lettuces, make the best fatting. The modes that are
resorted to by the French for fatting geese, *nailing*

them down by their webs, and other acts of cruelty, are, I hope, such as Englishmen will never think of. They will get fat enough without the use of any of these unfeeling means being employed. He who can deliberately inflict *torture* upon an animal in order to heighten the pleasure his palate is to receive in eating it, is an abuser of the authority which God has given him, and is, indeed, a tyrant in his heart. Who would think himself safe, if at the *mercy* of such a man?

DUCKS.

169. No water, to *swim* in, is necessary to the old and is *injurious* to the very young. They never should be suffered to swim (if water be near) till *more than a month old.* The old duck will lay, in the year, if *well kept*, ten dozen of eggs; and that is her best employment; for common hens are the best mothers. It is not good to let young ducks out in the morning to eat *slugs* and *worms;* for, though they like them, these things kill them if they eat a great quantity. Grass, corn, white cabbages and lettuces, and especially Buck-wheat, cut, when half ripe, and flung down in the haulm. This makes fine ducks. Ducks will feed on garbage and all sorts of filthy things; but, their flesh is *strong* and bad in proportion. They are, in Long Island, fatted upon a coarse sort of *crab*, called a horse-foot fish, prodigious quantities of which are cast on the shores. The young

ducks grow very fast upon this, and very fat; but, woe unto him that has to *smell* them when they come from the spit; and, as for *eating* them, a man must have a stomach indeed to do that!

170. When young they should be fed upon barley-meal, or *curds*, and kept in a warm place in the night time, and not let out *early* in the morning. They should, if possible, be kept from water to *swim* in. It always does them harm; and, if intended to be sold to be killed *young*, they should never go near ponds, ditches or streams.

TURKEYS.

171. These are *flying* things, and so are *common fowls*. But, it may happen, that a few hints respecting them may be of use. To raise turkeys in this chilly climate is a matter of much greater difficulty than in the climates that give great warmth. But, the great enemy to young turkeys (for old ones are hardy enough) is *the wet*. This they will endure in *no climate;* and so true is this, that, in America, where there is always " *a wet spell*" in April, the farmers' wives take care never to have a brood come out, until that spell is passed. In England, where the wet spells come at haphazard, the first thing is, to take care that young turkeys never go out, on any account, even in dry weather, till the *dew be quite off the ground;* and this should be adhered to, till they get to be of the size of an old partridge, and have

their backs well covered with feathers. And, in wet weather, they should be kept under cover all day long.

172. As to the *feeding* of them, when young, various nice things are recommended. Hard eggs, chopped fine, with crumbs of bread, and a great many other things; but, that which I have seen used, and always with success, and for all sorts of young poultry, is, milk *turned into curds*. This is the food for young poultry of all sorts. Some should be made *fresh every* day; and, if this be done, and the young turkeys kept warm, and especially *from wet*, not one out of a score will die. When they get to be strong, they may have meal and grain, but still they always love the curds.

173. When they get their *head feathers* they are hardy enough; and what they then want, is, *room*, to prowl about. It is best to breed them under a *common hen;* because she does not *ramble* like a hen-turkey; and, it is a very curious thing, that the turkeys, bred up by a hen of the common fowl, *do not themselves ramble much when they get old;* and, for this reason, when they buy turkeys for *stock*, in America (where there are such large woods and where the distant rambling of turkeys is inconvenient), they always buy such as have been bred under hens of the common fowl; than which a more complete proof of the great powers of *habit* is, perhaps, not to be found. And, ought not this to be a lesson to fathers and mothers of families? Ought

not they to consider, that the habits which they give their children, are to stick **by** those children during their whole lives?

174. The *hen* should be fed *exceedingly well* too, while she is *sitting* and *after* she has hatched ; for, though she does not give *milk*, she gives *heat ;* and, let it be observed, that, as no man ever yet saw healthy pigs with a poor sow; so no man ever saw healthy chickens with a poor hen. This is a matter much too little thought of in the rearing of poultry; but it is a matter of the greatest consequence. Never let a poor hen sit; feed the hen well while she is sitting; and feed her most abundantly when she has young ones; for then her *labour* is very great ; she is making exertions of some sort or other during the whole twenty-four hours ; she has no rest; is constantly doing something or other to provide food or safety for her young ones.

175. As to *fatting* turkeys, the best way is, never to let them be poor. *Cramming* is a nasty thing, and quite unnecessary. Barley-meal, mixed with skim-milk, given to them, fresh and fresh, will make them fat in a short time, either in a coop, in a house, or running about. Boiled carrots and Swedish turnips will help, and it is a change of sweet food. In France they sometimes *pick turkeys alive* to make them *tender ;* of which I shall only say, that the man that can do this, or order it to be done, ought to be skinned alive himself.

FOWLS

176. These are kept for two objects; their *flesh* and their *eggs*. As to *rearing them*, every thing said about rearing turkeys is applicable here. They are best *fatted*, too, in the same manner. But, as to *laying hens*, there are some means to be used to secure the use of them in *winter*. They ought not to be *old hens*. Pullets, that is, birds hatched in the foregoing spring, are, perhaps, the best. At any rate, let them not be more than *two years old*. They should be kept in a *warm* place; and not let out, even in the day time, in *wet* weather; for one good sound wetting will keep them back for a fortnight. The dry cold, even the severest cold, if *dry*, is less injurious than even a little *wet*, in winter time. If the feathers get wet, in our climate, in winter, or in short days, they do not get dry for a long time; and this it is that spoils and kills many of our fowls.

177. The French, who are great egg-eaters, take singular pains as to the *food* of laying hens, in winter. They let them out very little, even in their fine climate, and give them very stimulating food : barley boiled, and given them warm ; curds; *buckwheat* (which, I believe, is the best thing of all, except curds); parsley and other herbs chopped fine; leeks chopped in the same way; also apples and pears chopped very fine; oats and wheat cribbled; and sometimes they give them hemp-seed, and the

seed of nettles; or dried nettles, harvested in summer, and boiled in the winter. Some give them ordinary food, and, once a day, toasted bread sopped in wine. White cabbages chopped up are very good, in winter, for all sorts of poultry.

178. This is taking a great deal of pains; but, the produce is also great and very valuable in winter; for, as to *preserved* eggs, they are things to run *from* and not after. All this supposes, however, a proper *hen-house*, about which we, in England, take very little pains. The *vermin*, that is to say, the *lice*, that poultry breed, are their greatest annoyance. And, as our wet climate furnishes them, for a great part of the year, with no *dust* by which to get rid of these vermin, we should be very careful about *cleanliness* in the hen-houses. Many a hen, when sitting, is compelled to quit her nest to get rid of the lice. They torment the young chickens. And, in short, are a great injury. The fowl-house, should, therefore, be very often cleaned out; and sand, or fresh earth, should be thrown on the floor. The nests should not be on *shelves*, or on any thing fixed; but, little flat baskets, something like those that the gardeners have in the markets in London, and which they call *sieves*, should be placed against the sides of the house upon pieces of wood nailed up for the purpose. By this means the nests are kept perfectly clean, because the baskets are, when necessary, taken down, the hay thrown out, and the baskets washed; which cannot be done, if the nest

be made in any thing forming a part of the building. Besides this, the roosts ought to be cleaned every week, and the hay changed in the nests of laying hens. It is good to *fumigate* the house frequently by burning dry herbs, juniper wood, cedar wood, or with brimstone; for nothing stands so much in need of cleanliness as a fowl-house, in order to have fine fowls and plenty of eggs.

179. The *ailments* of fowls are numerous, but they would seldom be seen, if the proper care were taken. It is useless to talk of *remedies* in a case where you have complete power to prevent the evil. If well fed, and kept perfectly clean, fowls will seldom be sick; and, as to old age, they never ought to be kept more than a couple or three years; for they get to be good for little as layers, and no *teeth* can face them as food.

180. It is, perhaps, seldom that fowls can be kept conveniently about a cottage; but, when they can, three, four, or half a dozen, hens, to lay in *winter,* when the wife is at *home* the greater part of the time, are worth attention. They would require but little room, might be bought in November and sold in April, and six of them, with proper care might be made to clear every week the price of a gallon of flour. If the labour were great I should not think of it; but, it is *none*; and I am for neglecting nothing in the way of pains in order to insure a hot dinner, every day in winter, when the man comes home from work. This is the great thing to

think about; for, if there be not this, I defy the
Methodist Parson, or any other parson, to make the
family either happy or good. The laws relative to
poaching are quite terrible ; they make one shudder
to think of them; they form a code such as the
world never heard of before : but still, as a question
of economy, ten times as much is to be gained by
time spent in the care of tame animals as by the
time spent in the pursuit of wild ones. Several
little things amount to a great deal; and nothing,
lawfully within our power, ought to be neglected in
order to ensure comfort at home ; for without comfort there is *no home.*

PIGEONS.

181. A few of these may be kept about any cottage ; for they are kept even in towns by labourers
and artisans. They cause but little trouble. They
take care of their own young ones; and they do not
scratch, or do any other mischief in gardens. They
want feeding with Tares, Peas, or small Beans; and
Buck-wheat is very good for them. To *begin* keeping them, they must not have *flown at large* before
you get them. You must keep them for two or three
days, shut into the place which is to be their home ;
and then they may be let out, and will never leave
you as long as they can get proper food, and are
undisturbed by vermin, or unannoyed exceedingly
by lice.

182. The common dove-house pigeons are the best to keep. They breed oftenest, and feed their young ones best. They begin to breed at about *nine months old*, and, if well kept, they will give you eight or nine pair in the year. Any little place, a shelf in the cow shed; a board or two under the eaves of the house; or, in short, any place under cover even on the ground floor, they will sit and hatch and breed up their young ones in.

183. It is not supposed, that there could be much *profit* attached to them; but, they are of this use; they are very pretty creatures; very interesting in their manners; they are an object to delight *children* and to give them the *early habit* of fondness for animals and of *setting a value* on them, which, as I have often had to observe, is a very great thing. A considerable part of all the *property* of a nation consists of animals. Of course a proportionate part of the cares and labours of a people appertain to the breeding and bringing to perfection those animals; and, if you consult your experience, you will find, that a labourer is, generally speaking, of value in proportion as he is worthy of being entrusted with the care of animals. The most careless fellow cannot *hurt* a hedge or ditch; but to trust him with the *team*, or the *flock*, is another matter. And, mind, for the *man* to be trust-worthy in this respect, the *boy* must have been in the *habit* of being kind and considerate towards animals; and nothing is so likely to give him that excellent habit as his seeing, from

his very birth, animals taken great care of and treated with great kindness by his parents, and now-and-then having a little thing *to call his own.*

RABBITS.

184. In this case, too, the chief use, perhaps, is to give children those habits of which I have been just speaking. Nevertheless, Rabbits are really profitable. Three does and a buck will give you a rabbit to eat for *every three days in the year*, which is a much larger quantity of food than any man will get by spending half his time in the pursuit of *wild* animals, to say nothing of the toil, the tearing of clothes, and the danger of pursuing the latter.

185. Every body knows how to knock up a rabbit hutch. The Does should not be allowed to have more than *seven litters* in a year. Six young ones to a doe is all that ought to be kept; and then they will be fine. *Abundant food* is the main thing; and what is there that a rabbit will *not eat ?* I know of nothing *green* that they will not eat; and if hard pushed, they will eat *bark* and even wood. The best thing to feed the young ones on, when taken from the mother, is the *carrot*, wild or garden. Parsnips, Sweedish Turnips, roots of Dandelion; for, too much green or *watery* stuff is not good for *weaning*

H

rabbits. They should remain as long as possible with the mother. They should have oats once a-day; and, after a time they may eat any thing with safety. But, if you give them too much *green* at first when they are weaned, they *rot* as sheep do. A *variety* of food is a great thing; and, surely, the fields and gardens and hedges furnish this variety! All sorts of grasses, strawberry-leaves, ivy, dandelions, the *hog-weed*, or *wild parsnip*, in root, stem, and leaves. I have fed working horses, six or eight in number, upon this plant for weeks together. It is a tall bold plant that grows in prodigious quantities in the hedges and coppices in some parts of England. It is the *perennial parsnip*. It has flower and seed precisely like those of the parsnip; and hogs, cows, and horses are equally fond of it. Many a half-starved pig have I seen within a few yards of cart-loads of this pig-meat! This arises from want of the early habit of attention to such matters. I, who used to get hog-weed for pigs and for rabbits when a little chap, have never forgotten that the wild parsnip is good food for pigs and rabbits.

186. When the doe has young ones, feed her most abundantly with all sorts of greens and herbage and with carrots and the other things mentioned before, besides giving her a few oats once a-day. That is the way to have fine healthy young ones, which, if they come from the mother in good case, will very seldom die. But, do not think, that, because she is a small animal, a little feed is suffi-

cient! Rabbits eat a great deal more than cows or sheep in proportion to their bulk.

187. Of all animals rabbits are those that *boys* are most fond of. They are extremely pretty, nimble in their movements, engaging in their attitudes, and always completely under immediate controul. The produce has not long to be waited for. In short they keep an interest constantly alive in a little chap's mind; and, they really *cost nothing :* for, as to the *oats,* where is the boy that cannot, in harvest time, pick up enough along the *lanes* to serve his rabbits for a year? The *care* is all; and the habit of taking care of things is, of itself, a most valuable possession.

188. To those gentlemen who keep rabbits for the use of their family (and a very useful and convenient article they are) I would observe, that, when they find their rabbits die, they may depend on it, that ninety-nine times out of the hundred, *starvation* is the malady. And particularly short feeding of the doe, while, and before she has young ones ; that is to say, short feeding of her *at all times;* for, if she be poor, the young ones will be good for nothing. She will *live* being poor, but she will not, and cannot breed up fine young ones.

GOATS AND EWES.

189. In some places, where a cow cannot be kept a Goat may. A correspondent points out to me, that

H 2

a Dorset ewe or two might be kept on a common near a cottage to give milk; and certainly this might be done very well; but, I should prefer a goat, which is hardier, and much more domestic. When I was in the army, in New Brunswick, where, be it observed, the snow lies on the ground seven months in the year, there were many goats that *belonged to the regiment*, and that went about with it on ship-board and every where else. Some of them had gone through nearly the whole of the *American War*. We *never fed* them. In summer they picked about wherever they could find grass; and in winter they lived on cabbage-leaves, turnip-peelings, potatoe-peelings, and other things flung out of the soldiers' rooms and huts. One of these goats belonged to me, and, on an average throughout the year, she gave me more than three half pints of milk a day. I used to have the kid killed when a few days old; and, for some time, the goat would give nearly, or quite, two quarts of milk a day. She was seldom dry more than three weeks in the year.

190. There is one great inconvenience belonging to goats; that is, they bark all young trees that they come near; so that, if they get into a *garden*, they destroy every thing. But, there are seldom trees on commons, except such as are too large to be injured by goats; and I can see no reason against keeping a goat, where a cow cannot be kept. Nothing is so hardy; nothing so little nice as to its food. Goats will pick peelings out of the kennel and eat them.

They will eat mouldy bread or biscuit; fusty hay, and almost rotten straw; furze-bushes, heath, thistles; and, indeed, what will they not eat, when they will make a hearty meal on *paper*, brown or white, printed on or not printed on, and give milk all the while. They will lie in any dog-hole. They do very well clogged, or stumped out. And, then, they are very *healthy* things into the bargain, however closely they may be confined. When sea voyages are so stormy as to kill geese, ducks, fowls, and almost pigs, the goats are well and lively; and when a dog of no kind can keep the deck for a minute, a goat will skip about upon it as bold as brass.

191. Goats do not *ramble* from home. They come in regularly in the evening, and, if called, they come, like dogs. Now, though Ewes, when taken great care of, will be very gentle, and though their milk may be rather more delicate than that of the goat, the Ewes must be fed with nice and clean food, and they will not do much in the milk-giving way upon a common; and, as to *feeding them*, provision must be made pretty nearly as for a cow. They will not endure *confinement* like goats; and they are subject to numerous ailments, that goats know nothing of. Then the Ewes are done by the time they are about six years old; for they then lose their teeth; whereas a goat will continue to breed and to give milk in abundance for a great many years. The sheep is *frightened* at every thing, and especially at the least sound of a dog. A goat, on the

contrary, will *face a dog*, and, if he be not a big and courageous one, beat him off.

192. I have often wondered how it happened that none of our labourers kept goats; and I really should be glad to see the thing tried. They are pretty creatures, domestic as a dog, will stand and watch, as a dog does, for a crumb of bread, as you are eating; give you no trouble in the milking; and I cannot help being of opinion, that it might be of great use to introduce them amongst our labourers.

CANDLES AND RUSHES.

193. We are not permitted to make Candles ourselves, and, if we were, they ought seldom to be used in a labourer's family. I was bred and brought up mostly by *Rush-light*, and I do not find that I see less clearly than other people. Candles certainly were not much used in English labourer's dwellings in the days when they had meat dinners and Sunday coats. Potatoes and taxed candles seem to have grown into fashion together; and, perhaps, for this reason: that, when the pot ceased to afford *grease* for the rushes, the potatoe-gorger was compelled to go to the chandler's shop for light to swallow the potatoes by, else he might have devoured peeling and all

194. My grandmother, who lived to be pretty

nearly ninety, never, I believe, burnt a candle in
her house in her life. I know that I never saw one
there, and she, in a great measure, brought me up.
She used to get the meadow-rushes, such as they tie
the hop-shoots to the poles with. She cut them when
they had attained their full substance, but were still
green. The rush, at this age, consists of a body of
pith, with a green *skin* on it. You cut off both ends
of the rush, and leave the prime part, which, on an
average, may be about a foot and a half long. Then
you take off all the green skin, except for about a
fifth part of the way round the pith. Thus it is a
piece of pith all but a little strip of skin in one part
all the way up, which, observe, is necessary to hold
the pith together all the way along.

195. The rushes being thus prepared, the *grease*
is melted, and put, in a melted state, into something
that is as *long* as the rushes are. The rushes are
put into the grease; soaked in it sufficiently; then
taken out and laid in a bit of bark, taken from a
young tree, so as not to be too large. This bark is
fixed up against the wall by a couple of straps put
round it; and there it hangs for the purpose of holding the rushes.

196. The rushes are carried about *in the hand;*
but, to sit by, to work by, or to go to bed by, they
are fixed in *stands* made for the purpose, some of
which are high, to stand on the ground, and some
low, to stand on a table. These stands have an iron
part something like a pair of *pliers* to hold the rush

in, and the rush is shifted forward from time to time, as it burns down to the thing that holds it.

197. Now these rushes give a *better light* than a common small dip-candle; and they cost next to nothing, though the labourer may, with them, have as much light as he pleases, and though, without them, he must sit the far greater part of the winter evenings *in the dark*, even if he expend *fifteen shillings* a year in candles. You may do any sort of work by this light; and, if reading be your taste, you may read the foul libels, the lies and abuse, which are circulated gratis about *me* by the " Society for promoting *Christian Knowledge*," as well by rush-light as you can by the light of taxed candles; and, at any rate, you would have one evil less; for to be deceived and to pay a tax for the deception are a little too much for even modern loyalty openly to demand.

MUSTARD.

198. Why *buy* this, when you can *grow* it in your garden? The stuff you buy is half *drugs*, and is injurious to health. A *yard square* of ground, sown with common Mustard, the crop of which you would grind for use, in a little mustard-mill, as you wanted it, would save you *some money*, and probably save your *life*. Your mustard would look *brown* instead of *yellow;* but the former colour is as good as the

latter: and, as to the *taste*, the *real* mustard has certainly a much better than that of the *drugs* and flour, which go under the name of mustard. Let any one *try* it, and I am sure he will never use the drugs again. The drugs, if you take them freely, leave *a burning at the pit of your stomach*, which the real mustard does not.

DRESS, HOUSEHOLD GOODS, AND FUEL.

199. In paragraph 152, I said, I think, enough to caution you, the English labourer, against the taste, now too prevalent for *fine* and *flimsy* dress. It was, for hundreds of years, amongst the characteristics of the English people, that their taste was, in all matters, for things solid, sound, and good ; for the *useful*, the *decent*, the *cleanly* in dress, and not for the *showy*. Let us hope, that this may be the taste again ; and let us, my friends, fear no troubles, no perils, that may be necessary to produce a return of that taste, accompanied with full bellies and warm backs to the labouring classes.

200. In *household goods*, the *warm*, the *strong*, the *durable*, ought always to be kept in view. Oak tables, bedsteads and stools, chairs of oak or of yew-tree, and never a bit of miserable deal board. Things of this sort ought to last several lifetimes.

H 5

A labourer ought to inherit from his great grandfather something besides his toil. As to bedding, and other things of that sort, all ought to be good in their nature, of a durable quality, and plain in their colour and form. The plates, dishes, mugs, and things of that kind, should be of *pewter,* or even of wood. Any thing is better than crockery-ware. Bottles to carry a-field should be of wood. Formerly, nobody but the gipsies and mumpers, that went a hop-picking in the season, carried glass or earthern bottles. As to *glass* of any sort, I do not know, what business it has in any man's house, unless he be rich enough to live on his means. It pays a tax, in many cases, to the amount of two-thirds of its cost. In short, when a house is once furnished with sufficient goods, there ought to be no renewal of hardly any part of them wanted for half an age, except in case of destruction by fire. Good management in this way leaves the man's wages to provide an *abundance of good food and good raiment;* and these are the things that make happy families; these are the things that make a good, kind, sincere and brave people ; not little pamphlets about "loyalty" and "content." A good man will be contented, fast enough, if he be fed and clad sufficiently ; but, if a man be not well fed and clad, he is a base wretch to be contented.

201. *Fuel* should be, if possible, provided in summer, or at least some of it. Turf and peat must be got in summer, and some *wood* may. In the

woodland countries, the next winter ought to be thought of in *June*, when people hardly know what to do with the fuel-wood ; and something should, if possible, be saved in the bark-harvest to get a part of the fuel for the next winter. Fire is a capital article. To have no fire, or a bad fire, to sit by, is a most dismal thing. In such a state man and wife must be something out of the common way to be in good humour with each other, to say nothing of colds, and other ailments which are the natural consequence of such misery. If we suppose the great Creator to condescend to survey his works in detail, what object can be so pleasing to him as that of the labourer, after his return from the toils of a cold winter day, sitting with his wife and children round a cheerful fire, while the wind whistles in the chimney and the rain pelts the roof ? But, of all God's creation what is so miserable to behold or to think of as a wretched, half-starved family creeping to their nest of flocks or straw, there to lie shivering, till sent forth by the fear of absolutely expiring from want ?

HOPS.

202. I treated of them before ; but, before I conclude this little Work, it is necessary to speak of them again. I made a mistake as to the *tax* on the Hops. The positive tax is 2*d.* a pound, and I (in former editions) stated it at 4*d.* However in all such

cases, there falls upon the *consumer* the *expenses* attending the paying of the tax. That is, to say, the cost of interest of capital in the grower who pays the tax, and who must pay it, whether his hops be cheap or dear. Then the *trouble* it gives him, and the rules he is compelled to obey in the drying and bagging, and which cause him great *expense*. So that the tax on hops of our own English growth, may *now be reckoned* to cost the *consumer* about $3\frac{1}{4}d$. a pound.

YEAST.

203. Yeast is a great thing in domestic management. I have once before published a receipt for making *yeast-cakes*, I will do it again here.

204. In Long Island they make *yeast cakes*. A parcel of these cakes is made *once a year*. That is often enough. And, when you bake, you take one of these cakes (or more according to the bulk of the batch) and with them raise your bread. The very best bread I ever eat in my life was lightened with these cakes.

205. The materials for a good batch of cakes are as follows:—3 ounces of good fresh Hops; $3\frac{1}{2}$ pounds of Rye-Flour; 7 pounds of Indian Corn Meal; and one Gallon of Water.—Rub the hops, so as to separate them. Put them into the water, which is to be boiling at the time. Let them boil half an hour. Then strain the liquor through a fine sieve

160

into an earthen vessel. While the liquor is hot, put in the Rye-Flour; stirring the liquor well, and quickly as the Rye-Flour goes into it. The day after, when it is working, put in the Indian-Meal, stirring it well as it goes in. Before the Indian-Meal be all in, the mess will be very stiff; and, it will, in fact, be *dough*, very much of the consistence of the dough that bread is made of.—Take this dough; knead it well, as you would for *pie-crust*. Roll it out with a rolling-pin, as you roll out pie-crust, to the thickness of about a third of an inch. When you have it (or a part of it at a time) rolled out, cut it up into cakes with a tumbler-glass turned upside-down, or with something else that will answer the same purpose. Take a clean board (a *tin* may be better) and put the cakes *to dry in the sun.* Turn them every day; let them receive *no wet;* and they will become as hard as ship biscuit. Put them into a bag, or box, and keep them in a place *perfectly free from damp.*—When you bake, take two cakes, of the thickness abovementioned, and about 3 inches in diameter; put them into hot water, *over-night*, having cracked them first. Let the vessel containing them stand near the fire-place all night. They will dissolve by the morning, and then you use them in setting your sponge (as it is called) precisely as you would use the yeast of beer.

206. There are *two things*, which may be considered by the reader as obstacles. FIRST, where are *we* to get the *Indian-Meal?* Indian-Meal is

used merely because it is of a *less adhesive* nature than that of wheat. White pea-meal, or even barley-meal, would do just as well. But, Second, to *dry* the cakes, to make them (and *quickly* too, mind) as *hard as ship biscuit* (which is much harder than the timber of Scotch firs or Canada firs); and to do this *in the sun* (for it must not be *fire*), where are we, in this climate, to *get the sun?* In 1816 we could not; for, that year, melons rotted in the *glazed frames* and never ripened. But, in every nine summers out of ten, we have, in June, in July or in August, a *fortnight of hot sun ;* and that is enough. Nature has not given us a *peach-climate;* but we *get peaches.* The cakes, when put in the sun, may have a *glass sash*, or a *hand-light*, put over them. This would make their birth *hotter* than that of the hottest open-air situation in America. In short, to a farmer's wife, or any good housewife, all the little difficulties to the attainment of such an object would appear as nothing. The *will* only is required ; and, if there be not that, it is useless to think of the attempt.

SOWING SWEDISH TURNIP SEED.

207. It is necessary to be a little more full than I have been before as to the *manner of sowing* this seed ; and, I shall make my directions such as to be applied on a small or a large scale.—Those that

want to transplant on a large scale will, of course, as to the other parts of the business, refer to my larger work.—It is to get plants for *transplanting* that I mean to sow the Swedish Turnip Seed. The *time* for sowing must depend a little upon the nature of the situation and soil. In the north of England, perhaps early in April may be best; but, in any of these southern counties, any time after the *middle of April and before the* 10*th of May*, is quite early enough. The ground, which is to receive the seed, should be made very *fine*, and manured with wood-ashes, or with good compost well mixed with the earth. Dung is not so good; for it breeds the fly more; or, at least, I think so. The seed should be sown in drills *an inch deep*, made as pointed out under the head of *Sowing* in my book on *Gardening*. When deposited in the drills, *evenly* but *not thickly*, the ground should be raked across the drills, so as to fill them up; and then the whole of the ground should be *trod hard*, with shoes not nailed, and not very thick in the sole. The ground should be laid out in four-feet *beds* for the reasons mentioned in the " *Gardener*." When the seed come up, thin the plants to two inches apart as soon as you think them clear from the fly; for, if left thicker, they injure each other even in this infant state. Hoe frequently between the rows even before thinning the plants; and, when they are thinned, hoe well and frequently between them; for, this has a tendency to make them strong, and the hoeing *before thinning* helps to keep off the fly. A rod of ground, the rows being eight inches apart, and plants two inches apart in the row, will contain about *two thousand two hundred* plants. An acre, in rows four feet apart, and the plants a foot apart in the row, will take ten thousand and about four hundred and sixty plants. So that to transplant an acre, you must sow about *five rod of ground.* The plants should be kept very clean; and, by the last week in June, or first in July, you put them out. I have put them out (in England) at all times between 7th of June, and middle of August. The first is certainly earlier than I like; and the very finest I ever grew in England, and the finest I ever saw for a large piece, were transplanted on the 14th of July. But, one year with another, the last week in June is the best time.—For size of plants, manner of transplanting, intercultivation, preparing the land, and the rest, see " *Year's Residence in America,*" a new and *cheap* edition of which is now in the press.

No. VIII.

On the converting of English Grass, and Grain Plants cut green, into Straw, for the purpose of making Plat for Hats and Bonnets.

Kensington, 30 May, 1823.

208. THE foregoing Numbers have treated, chiefly, of the management of the affairs of a labourer's family, and more particularly of the mode of disposing of the money, earned by the labour of the family.

The present Number will point out what I hope may become *an advantageous kind of labour.* All along I have proceeded upon the supposition, that the wife and children of the labourer be, as constantly as possible, employed *in work of some sort or other.* The cutting, the bleaching, the sorting and the platting of straw, seem to be, of all employments, the best suited to the wives and children of country labourers ; and the discovery which I have made, as to the means of obtaining the necessary materials, will enable them to enter at once upon that employment.

209. Before I proceed to give my directions relative to the performance of this sort of labour, I shall give a sort of history of the discovery to which I have just alluded.

210. The practice of making Hats, Bonnets, and other things, of *straw,* is perhaps of very ancient date ; but, not to waste time in fruitless inquiries, it is very well known, that, for many years past, straw coverings for the head have been greatly in use in England, in America, and indeed in almost all the countries that we know much of. In this country the manufacture was, only a few years ago, *very flourishing;* but, it has now greatly declined, and has left in poverty and misery those whom it once well fed and clothed.

211. The cause of this change has been, the importation of the straw hats and bonnets from *Italy,* greatly superior, in durability and beauty, to those made in England. The plat made in England was made of the straw of *ripened grain.* It was, in general, *split ;* but, the main circumstance was, that it was made of the straw of *ripened grain ;* while the Italian plat was made of the straw of grain, or grass, *cut green.* Now, the straw of ripened grain or grass is brittle ; or, rather, rotten. It *dies* while standing, and, in point of toughness, the difference between it and straw from plants cut green is much about the

same as the difference between a stick that has *died on the tree* and one that has been *cut from the tree*. But, besides the difference in point of toughness, strength, and durability, there was the difference in beauty. The colour of the Italian plat was better; the plat was brighter; and the Italian straws being *small whole* straws, instead of small straws made by the splitting of large ones, there was a *roundness* in them, that gave *light and shade* to the plat, which could not be given by our flat bits of straw. In addition to these differences, there was, on our side, the further disadvantage of being compelled to use *brimstone* and other things, to bleach, or, rather, to clean and to give a colour to our straw. This caused the articles made of our straw to change colour when they came to face the rain and sun; while the Italian articles, though usually somewhat *clarified* in the same way, remained unchanged, because the straw of which they were composed had been cut green, and bleached by *scalding*.

212. It seems odd, that nobody should have set to work to find out how the Italians *came by* this fine straw. The importation of these Italian articles was chiefly from the port of LEGHORN; and, therefore, the bonnets imported were called, *Leghorn Bonnets.* The straw-manufacturers in this country seem to have made no effort to resist this invasion from Leghorn. And, which is very curious, the Leghorn *straw* has now begun to be imported, and to be *platted in this country.* So that we had *hands* to plat as well as the Italians. All that we wanted was the *same kind of straw*, that the Italians had: and it is truly wonderful, that these importations from Leghorn should have gone on increasing, year after year, and our domestic manufacture dwindling away at a like pace, without there having been any inquiry relative to the way in which the Italians *got their straw!* Strange, that we should have imported even *straw* from Italy, without inquiring whether

similar straw could not be got in England! There really seems to have been an opinion, that England could no more produce this straw than it could produce the sugar-cane.

213. Things were in this state, when, in 1821, a Miss WOODHOUSE, a farmer's daughter in CONNECTICUT, sent a straw-bonnet of her own making to the *Society of Arts* in London. This bonnet, superior in fineness and beauty to any thing of the kind that had come from Leghorn, the maker stated to consist of the straw of a sort of grass, of which she sent, along with the bonnet, some of the *seeds.* The question was, then, would these precious seeds *grow* and *produce plants in perfection in England?* A large quantity of the seed had not been sent; and it was therefore, by a Member of the Society, thought desirable to get, with as little delay as possible, a considerable quantity of this seed.

214. It was in this stage of the affair that my attention was called to it. The Member just alluded to applied to me to get the seed from America. I was of opinion that there could be no sort of grass in Connecticut, that would not, and that *did not*, grow and flourish in England. My son JAMES, who was then at New York, had instructions from me, in June 1821, to go to Miss WOODHOUSE, and to send me home an account of the matter. In September, the same year, I heard from him, who sent me an account of the cutting and bleaching, and also a specimen of the Plat and of the Grass of Connecticut. Miss WOODHOUSE had told the Society of Arts, that the grass she used was the *Poa Pratensis.* This is the *smooth-stalked meadow-grass.* The specimen sent home by my son appeared to be of this sort. So that it was quite useless to send for *seed.* It was clear, that we had *grass enough* in England, if we could but make it into straw as handsome as that of Italy.

215. Upon my publishing an account of what had

taken place with regard to the American Bonnet, *an importer of Italian straw* applied to me to know whether I would *undertake to import American straw.* He was in the habit of importing Italian straw, and of having it platted in this country; but, having seen the bonnet of Miss Woodhouse, he was anxious to get the American straw. This gentleman showed me some Italian straw, which he had imported, and, as the seed heads were on, I could see what plant the straw had been made of. · The gentleman who showed them to me, told me (and, doubtless, he believed) that the plant was one that *would not grow in England.* I, however, who looked at the straw with the eyes of a farmer, perceived that it consisted of dry *oat, wheat,* and *rye* plants, and of *Bennet* and other *common grass* plants.

216. This quite settled the point of *growth in England.* It was now certain that we had the plants in abundance; and, the only question that remained to be determined was, Had we SUN to give to those plants the beautiful colour which the American and Italian straw had? If that colour were to be obtained by *art,* by any chemical applications, we could obtain it as easily as the Americans or the Italians; but, if it were the gift of the SUN solely, here might be a difficulty that it was impossible for us to overcome. My experiments have proved that the fear of such difficulty was wholly groundless.

217. It was late in September 1821 that I obtained this knowledge, as to the kinds of plants that the foreign straw was made from. I could, at that time of the year, do nothing in the way of removing my doubts as to the *powers of our Sun* in the bleaching of grass; but, I resolved to do this when the proper season for it should return. Accordingly, when the next month of *June* came, I went into the country for the purpose. I made my experiments, and, in short, I proved to demonstration, that we had not only the *Plants,* but the *Sun*

also, necessary for the making of straw, yielding in no respect to that of America or of Italy. I think that, upon the whole, we have greatly the advantage of those countries; for, grass is more abundant in this country than in any other. It flourishes here more than in any other country. It is here in a greater variety of sorts; and for *fineness* in point of size, there is no part of the world which can equal what might be obtained from some of our *downs* merely by keeping the land ungrazed till the month of July.

218. When I had obtained the straw, I got some of it made into plat. One piece of this plat was equal in point of colour, and superior in point of fineness, even to the plat of the bonnet of Miss Wood-house. It seemed, therefore, now to be necessary to do nothing more than to *make all this well known to the country.* As the Society of Arts had interested itself in the matter, and as I heard that, through its laudable zeal, several *sowings of the foreign grass-seed* had been made in England, I communicated an account of my experiments to that Society. The first communication was made by me on the 19th of February last, when I sent to the Society, specimens of my straw and also of the plat. Sometime after this, I attended a Committee of the Society on the subject, and gave them a verbal account of the way in which I had gone to work.

219. The Committee had, before this, given some of my straw to certain *manufacturers* of plat; in order to see what it would produce. These manufacturers, with the exception of one, brought *such* specimens of plat as to induce, at first sight, any one to believe that it was nonsense to think of bringing the thing to any degree of perfection! But, was it *possible* to believe this? Was it possible to believe that it could *answer* to import straw from Italy, to pay a twenty per cent. duty on that straw, and to have it plat-

ted here; and, that it would *not answer* to turn into plat straw of just the same sort grown in England? It was impossible to believe *this;* but possible enough to believe, that persons now making profit by Italian straw, or plat, or bonnets, would rather that English straw should not come, to shut out the Italian, and to put an end to the Leghorn trade.

220. In order to show the character of the reports of those manufacturers, I sent some parcels of straw into Hertfordshire, and got back, in the course of five days, *fifteen specimens of plat.* These I sent to the Society of Arts on the 3d of April; and I here insert a copy of the Letter which accompanied them.

TO THE SECRETARY OF THE SOCIETY OF ARTS.

Kensington, April 3, 1823.

SIR,—With this letter I send you sixteen specimens of Plat, and also eight parcels of Straw, in order to show the sorts that the plat is made out of. The numbers of the plat correspond with those of the straw; but, each parcel of straw has two numbers attached to it, except in the case of the first number, which is the *wheat straw.* Of each kind of straw a parcel of the *stoutest* and a parcel of the *smallest* were sent to be platted; so that each parcel of the straw now sent, except that of the wheat, refers to *two of the pieces of plat.* For instance, 2 and 3 of the plat is of the sort of straw marked 2 and 3; 4 and 12 of the plat is of the sort of straw marked 4 and 12; and so on. These parcels of straw are sent in order that you may know the *kind* of straw, or, rather, of grass, from which the several pieces of plat have been made. This is very *material;* because, it is by those parcels of straw that the *kinds of grass* are to be known.

The piece of plat, *No.* 16, is *American;* all the rest are from my straw. You will see, that 15 is the *finest plat of all.* No. 7 is from the *stout* straws of the same *kind* as No. 15. By looking at the parcel of straw, Nos. 7 and 15, you will see what sort of grass this is. The next, in point of beauty and fineness combined, are the pieces Nos. 13 and 8 ; and, by looking at the parcel of straw, Nos. 13 and 8, you will see what sort of grass that is. Next comes 10 and 5, which are very beautiful too; and the sort of grass, you will see. is the *common bennet.* The wheat, you see, is too coarse ; and, the rest of the sorts are either *too hard,* or too *brittle.* I beg you to look at Nos. 10 and 5. Those appear to me to be the thing to supplant the Leghorn. The colour is good, the straws *work well,* they afford a great *variety of sizes,* and they come from the common *bennet grass,* which grows all over the kingdom, which is cultivated in all our fields, which is in bloom in the fair month of June, which may be grown as fine or as coarse as we please, and ten acres of which would, I dare say, make ten thousand bonnets. However, 7 and 15, and 8 and 13, are very good ; and they are to be got in every part of the kingdom.

As to *platters,* it is to be too childish to believe that they are not to be got, when I could send off these straws, and get back the plat, in the course of five days. Far *better work* than this would have been obtained, if I could have gone on the errand myself. What, then, will people not do, who regularly undertake the business for their livelihood.? .

I will, as soon as possible, send you an account of the manner in which I went to work with the grass. The card of plat, which I sent you some time ago, you will be so good as to give me back again sometime; because I have now not a bit of the American plat left.   I am, Sir,

Your most humble and
Most obedient Servant,
Wm. COBBETT.

221. I should observe, that these written communications of mine to the Society, *belong,* in fact, to it, and will be published in its Proceedings, a volume of which comes out every year; but, in this case, there would have been a *year lost* to those who may act in consequence of these communications being made public. The grass is to be got, in great quantities and of the best sorts, only in *June* and *July;* and the Society's volume does not come out until *December.* The Society has, therefore, given its consent to the making of the communications public through the means of this little work of mine.

222. Having shown what sort of plat could be produced from English grass-straw, I next communicated to the Society an account of the method which I pursued in the cutting and bleaching of the grass. The Letter in which I did this I shall here insert a copy of, before I proceed further. In the original the paragraphs were *numbered* from *one* to *seventeen:* they are here marked by *letters,* in order to avoid confusion, the paragraphs of the work itself being marked by *numbers.*

TO THE SECRETARY OF THE SOCIETY OF ARTS.

Kensington, April 14, 1823.

A.—Sir,—Agreeably to your request, I now communicate to you a statement of those particulars, which you wished to possess, relative to the specimens of Straw and of Plat, which I have, at different times, sent to you for the inspection of the Society

B.—That my statement may not come too abruptly upon those Members of the Society, who have not had an opportunity of witnessing the progress of this interesting inquiry, I will take a short review of the circumstances which led to the making of my experiments.

C.—In the month of June 1821, a gentleman, a

Member of the Society, informed me, by letter, that a Miss Woodhouse, a farmer's daughter of Weathersfield in Connecticut, had transmitted to the Society a straw-bonnet of very fine materials and manufacture; that this bonnet (according to her account) was made from the straw of a sort of grass called *poz pratensis;* that it seemed to be unknown, whether the same grass would grow in England; that it was desirable to ascertain whether this grass would grow in England; that at all events it was desirable to get from America some of the seed of this grass; and that, for this purpose, my informant, knowing that I had a son in America, addressed himself to me, it being his opinion, that, if materials, similar to those used by Miss Woodhouse, could by any means be *grown in England*, the benefit to the nation must be considerable

D.—In consequence of this application, I wrote to my son James (then at New York), directing him to do what he was able in order to cause success to the undertaking. On the receipt of my letter, in July, he went from New York to Weathersfield, (about a hundred and twenty miles); saw Miss Woodhouse, made the necessary inquiries; obtained a specimen of the grass and also of the plat, which other persons at Weathersfield, as well as Miss Woodhouse, were in the habit of making; and, having acquired the necessary information as to cutting the grass and bleaching the straw, he transmitted to me an account of the matter; which account, together with his specimens of grass and plat, I received in the month of September.

E.—I was now, when I came to see the specimen of grass, convinced that Miss Woodhouse's materials could be *grown in England;* a conviction, which, if it had not been complete at once, would have been made complete immediately afterwards by the sight of a bunch of bonnet-straw *imported from Leghorn,* which straw was shown to me by the importer, and

I

which I found to be that of two or three sorts of our common grass, and of oats, wheat and rye.

F.—That the grass, or plants, could be *grown in England* was, therefore, now certain, and indeed that they were in point of commonness next to the earth itself. But, before the grass could, with propriety, be called materials for bonnet-making, there was the *bleaching* to be performed; and it was by no means certain that this could be accomplished by means of an *English sun*, the difference between which and that of Italy or Connecticut was well known to be very great.

G.—My experiments have, I presume, completely removed this doubt. I think that the straw produced by me to the Society, and also some of the pieces of plat, are of a colour which no straw or plat can surpass. All that remains, therefore, is for me to give an account of the manner in which I cut and bleached the grass which I have submitted to the Society in the state of straw.

H.—First, as to the *season* of the year, all the straw, except that of one sort of couch grass, and the long coppice-grass, which two were got in Sussex, were got from grass cut in Hertfordshire on the 21st of June. A grass headland, in a wheatfield, had been mowed during the forepart of the day; and, in the afternoon, I went and took a handful here and a handful there out of the swaths. When I had collected as much as I could well carry, I took it to my friend's house, and proceeded to prepare it for bleaching according to the information sent me from America by my son; that is to say, I put my grass into a shallow tub, put boiling water upon it until it was covered by the water, let it remain in that state for ten minutes, then took it out, and laid it very thinly on a closely mowed lawn in a garden. But, I should observe, that, before I put the grass into the tub, I tied it up in small bundles, or sheaves, each bundle being about six inches through at the butt-end. This was necessary, in order to be able to take the grass, at the end of ten minutes, out of the water, without throwing it into a confused mixture as to tops and tails. Being tied up in little bundles, I could easily, with a prong, take it out of the hot water. The bundles were put into a large wicker basket, carried to the lawn in the garden, and there taken out, one by one, and laid in swaths as before mentioned.

I.—It was laid *very thinly;* almost might I say, that no stalk of grass covered another. The swaths were *turned* once a day. The bleaching was completed at the end of *seven days* from the time of scalding and laying out. June is a fine month. The grass was, as it happened, cut on the *longest day in the year;* and, the weather was remarkably fine and clear. But, the grass which I afterwards cut in Sussex, was cut in the first week in August; and, as to the weather, my journal speaks thus:

August 1822.

    2d.—Thunder and rain.—*Began cutting Grass.*
    3d.—Beautiful day.
    4th.—Fine day.
    5th.—Cloudy day—*Began scalding Grass, and laying it out.*
    6th.—Cloudy greater part of the day.
    7th.—Same weather.
    8th.—Cloudy, and rather misty.—*Finished cutting Grass.*
    9th.—Dry, but cloudy.
    10th.—Very close and hot.—*Packed up part of the Grass.*
    11th.—Same weather.
    12th.
    13th. } Same weather.
    14th.
    15th.—Hot and clear.—*Finished packing up Grass.*

K.—The grass cut in Sussex was as *well bleached* as that cut in Hertfordshire; so that it is evident that we never can have a summer that will not afford Sun sufficient for this business.

L.—The part of the straw used for platting is that part of the stalk which is *above the upper joint;* that part which is between the *upper joint* and the seed-

2

branches. This part is taken out, and the rest of the straw thrown away. But, the *whole plant must be cut and bleached;* because, if you were to take off, *when green*, the part above described, that part would wither up to next to nothing. This part must die in company with the whole plant, and be separated from the other parts after the bleaching has been performed.

M.—The time of cutting must vary with the seasons, the situation, and the sort of grass. The grass which I got in Hertfordshire, than which nothing can, I think, be more beautiful, was, when cut, generally in *bloom;* just in bloom. The *wheat* was in full bloom; so that, a good time for getting grass may be considered to be that when the *wheat is in bloom*. When I cut the grass in Sussex, the *wheat was ripe*, for reaping had begun; but, that grass is of a very backward sort, and, besides, grew in the *shade*, amongst coppice wood and under trees, which stood pretty thick.

N —As to the sorts of grass, I have to observe, generally, that in proportion as the colour of the grass is *deep;* that is to say, getting further from the *yellow* and nearer to the *blue*, it is of a deep and *dead yellow* when it becomes straw. Those kinds of grass are best, which are, in point of colour, nearest to that of wheat, which is a fresh pale green. Another hing is, the quality of the straw as to *pliancy* and *toughness*. Experience must be our guide here. I had not time to make a large collection of sorts; but, those which I have sent you contain three sorts which are proved to be good. In my letter of the 3d instant I sent you *sixteen* pieces of plat and *eight* bunches of straw, having the seed heads on, in order to show the sorts of grass. The sixteenth piece of plat was American. The first piece was from *wheat* cut and bleached by me; the rest from *grass* cut and bleached by me. I will here, for fear of mistake, give a list of the names of the several sorts of grass, the straw of which was sent with my letter of the 3d instant, referring to the numbers, as placed on the plat and on the bunches of straw.

Pieces of Plat.	Bunches of Straw.	Sorts of Grass.
No. 1.	... No. 1. ...	— Wheat.
2. 3. }	....2 and 3......	{ Melica Cærulea; or, Purple Melica Grass.
4. 12. }	....4 and 12.....	{ Agrostis Stolonifera; or Fiorin Grass; that is to say, one sort of Couch-grass.
5. 10. }	....5 and 10.....	{ Lolium perenne; or, Ray-grass.
6. 11. }	....6 and 11.....	{ Avena Flavescens; or, Yellow Oat grass.
7. 15. }	....7 and 15.....	{ Cynosurus Cristatus; or, Crested Dog's-tail grass.
8. 13. }	....8 and 13.....	{ Anthoxanthum Odoratum; or, Sweet-scented Vernal grass.
9. 14. }	....9 and 14.....	{ Agrostis Canina; or, Brown Bent grass.

O.—These names are those given at the Botanical Garden *at Kew*. But, the same English names are not, in the country, given to these sorts of grass. The *Fiorin* grass, the *Yellow Oat-grass*, and the *Brown-Bent*, are all called *couch grass;* except that the latter is, in Sussex, called *Red Robin*. It is the native grass of the *Plains* of Long Island; and they call it *Red Top*. The *Ray-grass* is the common field grass, which is, all over the kingdom, sown with clover. The farmers, in a great part of the kingdom, call it *Bent*, or *Bennet*, grass; and, sometimes it is called *Darnel-grass*. The *Crested Dog's-tail* goes, in Sussex, by the name of *Hendon-bent;* for what reason I know not. The *sweet-scented Vernal-grass* I have never, amongst the farmers, heard any name for. Miss Woodhouse's grass appears, from the *plants* that I saw in the Adelphi, to be one of the sorts of Couch-grass. Indeed, I am sure that it is a Couch-grass, if the plants I there saw came from her seed. My Son, who went into Connecticut, who saw the grass growing, and who sent me home a specimen of it, is now in England: he was with me when I cut the grass in Sussex; and he says, that Miss Woodhouse's was a Couch-grass. However, it is impossible to look at the specimens of straw and of plat, which I have sent you, without being convinced that there is no want of the raw material in England. I was, after first hearing of the subject, very soon convinced, that the grass grew in England; but, I had great doubts as to the capacity of our *sun*. Those doubts my own experiments have completely removed; but, then, I was not aware of the great effect of the *scalding*, of which, by the way, Miss Woodhouse had said nothing, and the knowledge of which we owe entirely to my son James's journey into Connecticut.

P.—Having thus given you an account of the time and manner of cutting the grass, of the mode of cutting and bleaching; having given you the best account I am able as to the sorts of grass to be employed in this business; and having, in my former communications, given you specimens of the Plat wrought from the several sorts of straw, I might here close my letter; but, as it may be useful to speak of *the expense* of cutting and bleaching, I shall trouble you with a few words relating to it. If there were a field of *Ray-grass*, or of *Crested Dog's-tail*, or any other good sort, and nothing else growing with it, the expense of *cutting* would be very little indeed, seeing that the *scithe* or *reap-hook* would do the business at a great rate. Doubtless there *will be* such fields; but, even if the grass have to be cut by the handful, my opinion is, that the expense of cutting and bleaching would not exceed *four-pence* for straw enough to make a large bonnet. I should be willing to contract to supply straw, at this rate, for half a million of bonnets. The *scalding* must constitute a considerable part of the expense; because there must be *fresh water* for every parcel of grass that you put in the tub. When water has scalded one parcel of cold grass, it will not scald another parcel. Besides, the scalding draws out the *sweet matter* of the grass, and makes the water the colour of that horrible stuff, called London porter. It would be very good, by-the-bye, to give to pigs. Many people give *hay-tea* to pigs and calves; and this is *grass-tea.* To scald a large quantity, therefore, would require means not usually at hand, and the scalding is an essential part of the business. Perhaps, in a large and very convenient farm-house, with a good brewing copper, good fuel and water handy, four or five women might scald a wagon load in a day; and a wagon would, I think, carry straw enough (in the rough) to furnish the means of making a thousand bonnets. However, the scalding *might* take place *in the field itself*, by means of a portable boiler, especially if water were at hand; and, perhaps, it would be better to carry the water to the field, than to carry the grass to the farm-house; for, there must be *ground to lay it out upon the moment it has been scalded*, and no ground can be so proper as the newly mowed ground where the grass has stood. The *space*, too, must be *large* for any considerable quantity of grass. As to all these things, however, the best and cheapest methods will soon be discovered when people set about the work with a view to profit

Q.—The Society will want nothing from me, nor from any body else, to convince it of the importance of this matter; but I cannot, in concluding these communications to you, Sir, refrain from making an observation or two on the consequences likely to arise out of these inquiries. The manufacture is one of considerable magnitude. Not less than about *five millions* of persons in this kingdom have a dress, which consists partly of manufactured straw; and a large part, and all the most expensive part, of the articles thus used, now come from abroad. In cases where you can get from abroad any article at *less expense than you can get it at home,* the wisdom of fabricating that article at home may be doubted. But, in this case, you get the raw material by labour performed at home, and the cost of that labour is not nearly so great as would be the cost of the mere carriage of the straw from a foreign country to this. If our own people had all plenty of employment, and that, too, more profitable to them and to the country, than the turning of a part of our own grass into articles of dress; then, it would be advisable still to import Leghorn bonnets; but, the facts being the reverse, it is clear, that whatever money, or money's worth things, be sent out of the country, in exchange for Leghorn bonnets, is, while we have the raw material here for next to nothing, just so much thrown away. The Italians, it may be said, take some of our manufactures in exchange: and let us suppose, for the purpose of illustration, that they take cloth from Yorkshire. Stop the exchange between Leghorn and Yorkshire, and, does Yorkshire *lose part of its custom?* No: for, though those who make the bonnets out of English grass, prevent the Leghorners from buying Yorkshire cloth, they, with the money which they now get, instead of its being got by the Leghorners, buy the Yorkshire cloth themselves; and they wear this cloth too, instead of its being worn by the people of Italy: aye, Sir, and many, now in rags, will be well clad, if the laudable object of the Society be effected. Besides this, however, why should we not *export* the articles of this manufacture? To America we certainly should; and I should not be at all surprised if we were to export them to Leghorn itself.

R.—Notwithstanding all this, however, if the manufacture were of a description to require, in order to give it success, the *collecting of the manufacturers together in great numbers,* I should, however great the wealth that it might promise, never have done any thing to promote its establishment. The contrary is, happily, the case: here all is not only performed. *by hand*, but by hand *singly*, without any combination of hands. Here there is no power of machinery or of chemistry wanted. All is performed out in the open fields, or sitting in the cottage. There wants no coal mines and no rivers to assist: no water-powers nor powers of fire. No part of the kingdom is unfit for the, business. Every where there are grass, water, sun, and women and children's fingers; and these are all that are wanted. But, the great thing of all is this: that, to obtain the materials for the making of this article of dress, at once so gay, so useful, and, in some cases, so expensive, there requires *not a penny of capital*. Many of the labourers now make their own straw-hats to wear in summer. Poor rotten things, made out of the straw of ripened grain. With what satisfaction will they learn, that straw, twenty times as durable, to say nothing of the beauty, is to be got from every hedge! In short, when the people are well and clearly informed of the facts, which I have, through you, Sir, had the honour to lay before the Society, it is next to impossible that the manufacture should not become general throughout the country. In every labourer's house a pot of water can be boiled. What labourer's wife cannot, in the summer months, find time to cut and bleach grass enough to give her and her children work for a part of the winter? There is no necessity for all to be *platters*. Some may cut and bleach only. Others may prepare the straw, as mentioned in paragraph L. of this letter. And, doubtless, as the farmers in Hertfordshire now sell their straw to the platters, grass collectors and bleachers and preparers would do the same. So that there is scarcely any country labourer's family that might not derive some advantage from this discovery; and, while I am convinced that this consideration has been by no means over-

I 5

looked by the Society, it has been, I assure you, the great consideration of all with,

Sir,

Your most obedient and

Most humble Servant,

Wᴍ. COBBETT.

---

223. Since writing the above Letter, several things have occurred to me which I did not before think of; and I have made some inquiries respecting the Leghorn Hats, Plat, and Straw, the result of which inquiries it may be useful to communicate to my readers. In treating of a matter like this, it is very difficult to make oneself clearly understood, unless one *repeat* a good deal; and yet, to be clearly understood is the main thing, because here is to be no effect at all produced, or a real practical effect: people are, by this Treatise of mine, to be induced to spend their time, or money, or both, in the cutting of grass, and the bleaching of it; or, I write in vain. Unpleasant as repetition is, I must therefore repeat, rather than run the risk of not being understood. The heads, under each of which there remains something to be explained, or observed on, are: The *Sorts* of Grass or Grain; the *Season* for Cutting; the *Act of Cutting;* the *Act of Bleaching;* the *Housing* of the Straw; the *Pulling* of the Straw; the *Platting;* the *Knitting* of the Plat together; the *Cost,* to the importer, of the Leghorn Hats, Plat, and Straw.

224. SORTS OF GRASS OR GRAIN.—The PLATE, which I insert here, exhibits a pretty good representation of three sorts of Grass, just at the season when they are coming out into bloom. Figure 1. is the *Sweet-scented Vernal Grass;* Fig. 2. the *Crested Dog's Tail;* and Fig. 3. the *Bennet Grass,* or *Ray* Grass. At the Office of the Register, No. 183, Fleet-street, these may be seen in nature: little bunches

of them, in straw, that was harvested by me. However, by attentively looking at this Plate, any one may soon learn to distinguish these sorts from others. But, the reader is not to conclude, that these are the *only* sorts that will answer the purpose; nor, indeed, is he to conclude, that they are the *best* sorts that can be found. They are the best that I have yet found. They make, as may be seen by the specimens in Fleet-street, very fine and beautiful straw; but, amongst the great multitude of sorts of grass, I, or others, may possibly find other sorts as well or better suited to the purpose. The grass made use of by Miss Woodhouse is, unquestionably, the common Couch Grass. It is a great mistake to suppose, that there is any sort of grass growing in Connecticut, which does not also grow in England. Miss Woodhouse, in her communication to the Society of Arts, called her grass the *Poa Pratensis*. This is the smooth-stalked meadow-grass of England, and this is one of the most common grasses that grows in England. But Miss Woodhouse could only tell the name that was given to her; and it appears pretty evident to me, that the person who gave her the name to send to the Society, mistook the *Agrostis Vulgaris* for the *Poa Pratensis*. The former is, in its seed head, very much like the latter, only on a smaller scale. The *Agrostis Vulgaris* is our *common Couch Grass*, to extirpate which from our fields, or, rather, to keep it in check, costs millions of money every year. It was certainly not necessary to send to Connecticut for the seed of this greatest of all the curses of English agriculture. In some parts of England, particularly in Suffolk and Norfolk, this wicked grass is called *Spear Grass*, and that is the very name which Miss Woodhouse's grass goes by in Connecticut. Doubtless the name went out with the first settlers from the eastern part of England. They found the same sort of grass there that they had left behind them, and they gave it the same name. The *Couch Grass* has a finer stalk than the smooth-stalked meadow-grass. It is also very tough; and this was probably the reason for selecting it in Connecticut.

225. But, there are many other sorts of grass. The *yellow oat-grass*, particularly, is very fine; I think the finest of all. A specimen of the straw of this grass may be seen at 183, Fleet-street. This straw would make plat a great deal finer than that of the bonnet of Miss Woodhouse. Not only finer, but a great deal finer. Perhaps it is not more than half the size of the straw made use of by Miss Woodhouse, while the colour is as beautiful as it possibly can be. It is not, however, of the straw of *grass* only, or even principally, that I have to speak. None of the immense quantity of hats and plat imported from Leghorn, is made of the straw of grass. The Leghorn manufacture is made of the straw of *grain*, and principally of the straw of *wheat*, which, though not nearly so fine, in point of size, as the straw of many kinds of grass, is, perhaps, in point of colour, equal to the straw of even the best sorts of grass. This is what the Italians make their plat of. This is the material of which all those thousands upon thousands of bonnets are made that we see upon women's heads in England! How astonishing, then, is it, that English manufacturers in straw should have fallen into beggary, supposing all the while, that they could not make plat like that of the Italians for want of the materials to make it of, or for want of sun sufficiently bright to bleach those materials! The simple facts are these: the Leghorn bonnets are made of *wheat straw;* but, this straw comes from plants that are very fine and spindling in consequence of their standing very thick upon the ground; and, this Italian wheat is cut while it is *green* instead of remaining till it be dry. This makes it tough, instead of being rotten; and the smallness of the stalk enables the platters to make fine plat of

the *whole* round straw, instead of making use of the straw when split.

226. I believe, that some sorts of oats would do very well. It is not impossible that barley might do. Rye, I should imagine, would be very good ; but it is a fact that the Italians generally make use of wheat. If I were to sow wheat for the purpose, or indeed any other grain, I would sow about fifteen Winchester bushels to the statute acre. That, I should think, would give me the straw fine enough. If you sow wheat for the purpose, recollect, that there are some sorts of wheat which have a brown straw, and some sorts which have a white straw. The Italians sow, I believe, very frequently, the *spring-wheat*, for this purpose. I mean the spring *bearded* wheat. This sort of wheat has a very white straw ; and it may be sown at the same time that barley is sown. But I think that the sort of wheat that I should choose is that sort, which they call, in Hampshire, the *old fashioned white straw*, which has a small brown grain ; but the flour of which, and the straw of which, are whiter than those of any other kind of wheat. This is a winter wheat. It must be sown in the fall of the year ; and, the straw would probably be the tougher and brighter, if the land were a good stiff loam upon a bottom of chalk, great quantities of which land are found in Hertfordshire, the north of Hampshire, and divers other parts of the kingdom. I have often remarked, that if the land be of a loose texture, the straw of the wheat is seldom bright and sound. The finest and brightest straw that I ever saw in England, came from wheat which grew on a bed of almost solid clay. The straw was small enough, to be sure, and the ears short enough ; but the straw was the whitest and brightest that I ever saw stand upon any land in England.

227. An acre of wheat, would yield a prodigious quantity of straw ; and as to the straw being as good

for the purpose of making plat as is the straw which is grown in Italy, I have *demonstrated* the affirmative of the fact. I have left nothing for conjecture. I have left nothing to dispute about. I have gone into an English field. I have cut the wheat in that field. I have bleached it in English sun. I have then clarified it, after the manner of the Italians. I now offer for public inspection, at No. 183, Fleet-street, a bunch of this straw placed by the side of a bunch of straw imported from Italy. The Italian straw is from the spring wheat; my straw is from winter wheat. The eye can hardly be fixed upon any thing of the straw kind more bright and beautiful than these samples; but if there be any difference, the English wheat has produced the most beautiful straw. After this, I trust we shall hear no more about the importing of the *seeds of foreign plants*, for the purpose of raising bonnet straw. I do not blame those who have imported the seeds even of couch-grass. They could not know that the importation was not necessary. The importation could *do no harm*. But, it would do a great deal of harm to make people believe that it was necessary now to wait for the bringing of any *foreign* plant to perfection. I have demonstrated (and this is the great merit of the thing) that we have all the materials already in England; that we have every plant which the Italians and the Americans have, only that we have them, as far as relates to all sorts of grass, in greater perfection, and in greater abundance.

228. THE SEASON FOR CUTTING THE PLANTS.—I have before observed, that I cut my wheat and collected my grass in Hertfordshire, just at the time when the wheat was in full bloom. Upon further inspection of my wheat straw, I am of opinion that a better rule than that of the existence of the full bloom may be adopted. I have observed, in paragraph L. of my Letter to the Society, of the 14th of April, that no part of the straw is used for

platting, except that part of the stalk, which you find between the *upper joint* and the *seed-head*, or tassel, or bunch of flowers, or, to speak in the language of the Botanists, the *panicle.* When the straw has been bleached in the sun, you pluck the top part of the stalk out of the upper joint. Now, if the stalk be *round* and *full* at the part where it meets at the upper joint, the plant appears to me to be at the proper age ; but if it be not round and full where it meets at the upper joint, then it appears not to be quite ripe enough. If you pluck upwards a wheat plant, taking hold of the ear, you will not find the plant give way at the root ; but you will find the upper part of it come away, the separation being at the upper joint. Now, if the straw, or, rather, the stalk, be round, full, and tough, down in the socket, where the separation takes place, then it appears to me that the plant is far enough advanced ; but it certainly is not far enough advanced, if that part of the stalk which comes out of the socket, be soft, watery, and easily pinched asunder. This appears to me to be a very safe rule ; and it holds good with regard to the plants of grass, as well as with regard to the plants of grain. This is the best way of determining the season for cutting ; because, it applies to every kind of plant individually, and if it be well attended to, it will be impossible that much injury should arise to any party from cutting the grass or grain out of season. The season of the year when the several plants come to perfection may be seen by referring to the work of the greatest authority, called HORTUS KEWENSIS. But Mr. AITON, the King's gardener, has published an Epitome of this work, which is quite sufficient for all useful purposes. It contains *an account of every plant which is grown in the Botanical Garden at Kew ;* that is to say, *every plant of which the Botanists of Europe have any knowledge :* giving, at one view, the Botanical name and the English name, of every plant, a list of the different species, together with the following particulars annexed to each species: first, a reference to some book in which the figure of it is drawn; second, the country from which it is brought, if an exotic; third, the time when first known, if of modern discovery; and, which is more particularly useful to our present purpose, the *time of flowering*. So that nothing can be more useful, as well as entertaining; and I owe it especially to those of my readers who are zealous in promoting the object of this present Number of "Cottage Economy," to point out so compendious a source of information.

229. THE MANNER OF CUTTING.—I have already said that the plants may be mowed. Indeed, it signifies not with what instrument they be severed from the earth, provided they be properly collected together. For the cutting of grass by a handful at a time, I had a small reap-hook made, which was fastened to the end of a straight handle about a foot and a half long. With the hook in one hand, the woman that was using it collected, into her other hand, a good quantity of the *tops* of the grass. Holding these in one hand, she, with her hook, cut off the stalks as close to the ground as possible. Then, lifting up her grass, she gave the butts of it a rap with the back of her hook, and thus shook away the *undergrowth*, and every thing that did not belong to the stalks, the tops of which she held in her hand. For some time I had these handfuls of grass *tied at the butts in separate handfuls*. This operation being rather tedious, I afterwards had the grass tied in little bundles; but I am by no means certain, that, in the end, any time was saved by this more hasty manner of proceeding. Tied up in little handfuls, all the subsequent operations became easy in the extreme; and though my experience is not sufficient to induce me to speak very positively upon the subject, I am much disposed to think, that, where the grass is cut by handfuls, to tie it up in handfuls is the best way. In general, and especially in case of fields

of grain, the severing will, of course, take place by the scythe or the reap-hook. The latter, most likely, a great deal the best; because, in this case, strings would be laid out upon the land to receive the grips of green wheat, as bonds are laid out to receive the grips of ripe wheat. All those who may wish to procure platting straw may not be husbandmen; and therefore I ought here to observe, that the grips are the little parcels of wheat which the reapers lay down upon the ground as they are proceeding with their work. When these are bound up, they are called *sheaves;* and in their former state they are called *grips,* because, they consist of little parcels which the reaper has *gripped* in his hand, in going from the one side of his work to the other. In cutting the wheat, rye, and oats, or even grass, if it stood out in the clear in a field, the reaper would take grips in the same manner as if he were cutting ripe wheat. Strings, instead of bonds, would be laid upon the cleared ground to receive the grips; and one woman would cut and tie up with the greatest neatness, and with two ties to a grip, a quarter of an acre of grass in a day. While she was doing this, others would be employed in taking away the grass or the grain plants, scalding them, and laying them out to bleach. These would have to be turned, as we have seen. But, as to the division of labour, that would take care of itself, in a very short time. The expense of cutting would be very little; especially when we consider the quantity of plat that would be produced from an acre of land.

230. THE MANNER OF BLEACHING.— I have not much to add, upon this subject; except that I think it necessary to press upon the reader, that great care must be taken about the *scalding.* It is not the Italian sun and the American sun that has given those countries the fine and tough straw. We have finer grass than either of them; and we can have as fine straws of grain.

Our sun is also quite sufficient for the purpose; and, I believe, better than a hotter sun; but, the *scalding* we knew nothing about till we got the knowledge of it from Connecticut. Miss Woodhouse did not communicate this secret to the Society of Arts. Doubtless the girls of Connecticut had the secret communicated to them by some one that had been in Italy. When I sent to Connecticut to inquire about the seed, I instructed my son James to make inquiries into every thing concerning the matter. Thus it was that he came at the knowledge of the scalding, without which all the rest of the knowledge relating to the subject would be useless. On Monday, the 26th of this month of May, I cut two handfuls of grass, in my ground at Kensington, of the sort called, by the Botanists, *Alopecurus Pratensis*, or Meadow Fox-tail grass. One of the handfuls was scalded, and the other was not. Both were laid out upon the grass to bleach. On Wednesday night, that is to say, at the end of about two days and a half, the two parcels were taken in. The one not scalded was still *nearly green*, and the one that was scalded was *as white as wheat straw generally is at harvest.* These two samples may be seen by any body, at the Office of the Register, in Fleet Street. The grass was in bloom: it is a coarse grass, wholly unfit for platting; but it was the forwardest in my meadow, and it was as good as any other for the purpose of demonstrating the *effect of scalding.* This is the great secret of all; and I cannot help repeating the remark, which I have made elsewhere, how curious it is, that this secret should have been kept from us here in England until long after it had been communicated to the farmers' daughters in Connecticut. Any body who lives in the country, can try the effect of the scalding at any moment. Those who wish to see the effect, and have not an opportunity of being in the country, may see it by calling at the Office of the

Register. But, besides this bleaching in the sun, the Italians and the Americans also make use of a *clarifying* by the means of brimstone. All the Leghorn Plat and Leghorn Straw and Hats that are imported, are clarified by brimstone. My Son found that the same was practised in Connecticut; and, when straw bonnets are *cleaned* in England, they are cleaned by the means of brimstone. All the split straw is clarified by brimstone. My own opinion is, that we have some grass that will make plat even more beautiful without this clarifying, than any other thing will make with clarifying. But this is a matter of little interest. The Italians clarify the whole of their manufacture with brimstone; and, in that article, we do not yield to them at any rate. This clarifying is the easiest thing imaginable. The straw, the plat, or the bonnet, is wetted a little with clean cold water, which is then shaken off from it, leaving it in a wettish state. It is then shut up in a tub, in a box, in a cupboard, or in some place with some brimstone put into a little pan, and set upon the bottom of the box or tub, and set fire to. This is all that is necessary. This gives to the straw or plat or bonnet a very brilliant colour certainly; but a colour which I think may be surpassed without the use of brimstone. However, this is of no consequence at all; all that I pretend to is, to show that we can get in England, from our own fields, and our own grain and grass, materials for platting as fine and as good as can be obtained in Italy or in Connecticut.

231. THE HOUSING OF THE ROUGH STRAW.—In speaking of that part of bleaching which consists of clarifying, I might have observed, that the clarifying is a thing not to be bestowed upon any part of the plant, except that which is really for use. That part, therefore, of which I have spoken in paragraph L of my Letter of the 14th of April, is, of course, to be pulled or plucked from the rest of

the plant, and to be trimmed and got ready for use before it be clarified; for it would be useless to clarify the seed-heads and the bottoms of the plants, by way of preparation for the litter heap, or the bed of the farm-yard. But, before this pulling or plucking take place, the straw must be *housed* in its rough state; that is to say, it must be put away in a barn or granary, or some other safe and convenient place. For this purpose it should be tied up in neat and smooth bundles; and I am satisfied that it would answer the end of the proprietor to have it tied up in coarse stuff like hop-sacking, which would keep dust away from it, and protect it from various other injuries. At any rate, it should not be tied up unless *perfectly dry*. If not perfectly dry it will mould, or at any rate, grow damp; perhaps *heat* a little; and in either of these cases all your labour is thrown away. Care should be taken, besides, that the place where it is deposited be perfectly dry. Not only must there be no wet fall upon the straw; but there must be no dampness in the floor or in the walls of the building. A good dry barn might do very well: a malt-kiln, a hop-kiln, a granary, or, for a small quantity, a room in a house, which room has a boarded floor.

232. THE PULLING OF THE STRAW— That is to say, the act of taking the useful part from the other parts of the plant. The labours, of which I have hitherto spoken, are of a bustling kind, and are to be performed chiefly out of doors. This pulling of the straw may be performed by the fire-side. The way to go to work might be this. Here, I should say to a labouring man's wife, is a bundle of rough straw, weighing ten pounds. I have found, by experience, that every ten pounds of *rough straw* yield two pounds of *pulled straw*. Take this bundle, bring me back two pounds of pulled straw, and I give you so much money. The pulled straw would have the *seed-heads*, or *panicles*, on it; and would

probably be sold, in that state, to the platters, or the employers of the platters. That is the state *in which the straw is now imported from Italy.* What a curious thing! that we should be importing from Italy things which are so common in our own country, that we can hardly move about that country without actually treading upon these things! In all probability the course of the business will, in general, be this: one person will grow the plants, and harvest the straw. Another will purchase the rough straw of him, have it pulled, and sell the pulled straw to the platters, who will, as they now do in the case of the split straw, carry the plat to market and sell it. This appears to me likely to be the course of the trade; but the women in labourer's, farmer's, country tradesmen's, and even in gentlemen's houses, will make collections of grass for themselves. They will find out, I warrant them, those sorts of grass, which, when turned into bonnets, make a face look prettiest. There will not remain many banks and hedges in the kingdom unexplored for the purpose of discovering grass wherewith to make rare and beautiful straw. This is peculiarly an affair of the Women; and I never yet knew any thing to fail that they set about with a hearty good will.

233. THE PLATTING.—There will scarcely be any difficulty in finding people to plat English straw, seeing that there are enough already found to plat the Leghorn straw, imported into this country. This work has been for some time carried on by the industrious and most praiseworthy inhabitants of the Orkney Islands. Some persons in those islands have, at this time, some small parcels of my straw; and I expect samples of their plat in about a month's time. But, there will platters be found in all parts of the kingdom. If those who have been accustomed to plat the soft split straw, were, from some whim or other, to object to work upon the new manufacture, other platters would rise up to supply their

place. There will be too many persons interested in converting our own straw into plat, to suffer the manufacture to fail for want of persons to work in it.

234. THE KNITTING OF THE PLAT TO-GETHER.—The English straw plat is put together as boards are put on the side of a barn; that is to say, the plat, or lists of plat, are made one to cover a part of the other; and they are sewed through and through, the needle and thread performing the office of the nails in the case of the barn. Not thus is it with the Leghorn hats and bonnets. In order to make these, the plat is not lapped, a part of one list over a part of the other; but the lists are fastened to each other after the manner, or form, of boards put together by glew; that is to say, the *edge* of one list of plat is fastened to the edge of another list; and thus throughout the whole bonnet, just as boards, joined on to the edges of each other, form a table; and so neatly and so cleverly is this work of knitting the lists of plat performed, that you can no more discover the joinings of the plat in the one case, than you can the joinings of the boards in the other case. This is called knitting the plat; and there are at present, as far as I understand, not many persons in England, and those who are here are principally foreigners, who know how to do this business. Now, then for the honour of the Girls of Old England! Shall we be compelled to send young fellows to Italy and Con-necticut to fetch us Italians and Yankees to carry on this work of knitting together plat made of English straw? Recollect, the Yankee girls found out the way to knit the plat together. There were no foreigners to go to do the work for them or to teach them to do it. There is Miss Woodhouse's Bonnet at the apartments of the Society of Arts. That bonnet is knit together after the Italian manner; and am I to have the cruel mortification of hearing

one single English woman express a doubt of her being able to do the same thing ?

285. THE COST, TO THE IMPORTER, OF LEGHORN PLAT AND STRAW.—The Plat, which is imported from Leghorn in the shape of plat, pays a duty of seventeen shillings the pound weight, and stands the importer in about sixty shillings a pound, altogether. The plat which is imported in the form of hats, pays a duty of five and eight pence per hat, unless the hat exceed twenty-two inches in diameter, and then the duty is double. What the prime cost of the hat is, when bought in Italy, and what the amount of the freight and insurance, I cannot say. Of Leghorn *straw* no great quantity appears to have been imported. Some, however, is imported, and it pays a duty of twenty per cent.; and probably stands the importer, all charges included, in *three, four,* or *five* shillings a pound. Now, I will pledge myself to furnish any quantity of straw of any degree of fineness, not finer than hog's bristles, to persons ready to contract with me for it. I should not be afraid to say that I would furnish straw, equal in all respects to Leghorn straw, for less than half the price which Leghorn straw costs. How cheaply, then, can such straw be furnished by persons who live in the country, who have the land, the grass, the grain, the barns, and, into the bargain, the labouring people, all ready to their hand !

---

236. In conclusion, I have to observe, that, I by no means send forth this Essay as containing opinions and instructions that are to undergo no alteration. I am, indeed, endeavouring to teach others; but I am myself only a learner. Experience will, doubtless, make me much more perfect in a knowledge of the several parts of the subject; and the fruit of this experience I shall be careful to communicate to the

public. I am strongly disposed to believe that the manufacture, the establishment of which I am endeavouring to promote, will be beneficial to my country in many respects, and particularly, that it will tend to better the lot of the labouring classes ; to cause them to live better than they now live ; to give them better food and better raiment than they now have ; and to assist in driving from their minds the effects of that pernicious and despicable cant which has long been dinning into their ears, that hungry bellies and ragged backs are marks of the grace of God. At the time when I was leaving a felons' gaol, in which I had been imprisoned for two years for having expressed my indignation at the flogging of Englishmen in the heart of England, under a guard of Hanoverian bayonets ; at that time, in answer to some gentlemen, who presented me with an address, congratulating me on the preservation of my health, and expressing their indignation at the fine of a *thousand pounds* which I had just paid, and at the bonds for *seven years* into which I had been compelled to enter, my observation to those gentlemen was, that I should always remember this treatment, but that *the only way in which I should seek to be revenged of my enemies, was by rendering services to that Country of which they were the insolent oppressors.*

Printed and Published by J. M. Cobbett, No. 183, Fleet-street.

MR. COBBETT'S PUBLICATIONS.

PUBLISHED BY

J. M. COBBETT, 183, FLEET STREET, LONDON.

1. THE POLITICAL REGISTER—Is published in Two Editions, the one, price Sixpence, not having any stamp, cannot go postage free, and, therefore, is to be obtained in the country by those only who live in or near large Towns, to which parcels are sent. But, for the convenience of those who are to be reached in no other way than by cross-posts, a Stamped Edition is published, and may be obtained as newspapers are. The Stamped Edition is One Shilling.— Any of the *back Volumes*, of recent date, may be had by application at the Office as above.

2. COLLECTIVE COMMENTARIES.—This work contains all the *Commentaries*, published, in the STATESMAN NEWSPAPER, during the last Session of Parliament. To the Commentaries is added a *List of the Acts*, which were passed during the Session, with short remarks on those Acts which appeared to require them. This work states the result of all the *Divisions* upon questions of importance. It contains a notice of all the arguments, on both sides, upon every such question. It is a good *history of the Session.* It enables the reader to *look back*, and to see how men acted, and what opinions they maintained. It lies in a reasonable compass. It is a neat Octavo Volume of *great utility.* It is printed in a way that enables one to read it without destruction to eyes. And, it is sold for *Six Shillings.*—The work will be continued.

3. LONG ISLAND PROPHECIES.—This is a reprint of three "*Twopenny Trashes*," written while the Author was in *Long Island*, where he used his *long arm*, and kept himself out of the reach of SIDMOUTH. These *Prophecies* contain the Author's opinions as to what would happen to the country in case there were a *return to cash-payments without an adjustment of contracts.* If he had written *now*, instead of *five years* ago, his description of the consequences could not have been more exact. When he wrote those Prophecies, and sent them for publication in England (where they were published), he said: "Upon these Prophecies I *pledge my reputation* as a politician." They have been fulfilled to the very letter. This was his great and distinct *challenge* to the Ministry, the Parliament, and the London Press.—Price *Sixpence.*

4. PAPER AGAINST GOLD.—This is the history of that grand *mystery of iniquity*, the *Funding System.* It was written in 1810 and 1811, when the Author had been sent to *Newgate* for two years, with a *thousand pounds fine*, and *seven years* recognizances on his head, for having expressed his indignation at the flogging of *Englishmen* in the town of Ely, under a guard of *German* bayonets. It was after GIBBS had prosecuted him for this, and after ELLENBOROUGH, GROSE, LE BLANC, and BAILEY had passed this terrible sentence on him. It was while he was in prison, in consequence of this sentence, that he set steadily to work to tear up by the very roots, that system of *funding* and of

paper-money, the ultimate consequences of which he, then, clearly showed. This work contains the real *foundation* of all practical knowledge on this subject. The author saw, at that distant day, how necessary this knowledge would be to the nation; and he made provision accordingly. This book has passed through many editions. Every *young* man should read it. Price *Five Shillings*. A Stereotype Edition.

5. ENGLISH GRAMMAR. This work, written in Long Island, and published in America and in England, in the year 1818, has gone through several Editions, and has sold to the amount of about fifty thousand copies, without ever having been mentioned in any review and without scarcely any advertisement except in the Author's own publications. He ventures to say that, from this book any person however illiterate, will be enabled to write correctly in less time than is generally bestowed upon learning the first rudiments of spelling. Numerous are the instances in which even gentlemen have told me, that, though they had had what is generally called a liberal education, they had learnt more of grammar from his book in a month, than they had ever learnt before in all their lives. It is entitled, "A Grammar intended for the use of Schools and of Young Persons " in general; but more especially for the use of Soldiers, Sailors, " Apprentices and Ploughboys." But it has now, in this New Edition, an additional part, containing *"Six Lessons to Statesmen,"* to warn them against bad writing. These Lessons contain commentaries on the speech of the late Speaker of the House of Commons, which speech was addressed to the Regent on the subject of PEEL's Bill. It also contains commentaries on the Regent's Speech; on diplomatic writings of Lord CASTLEREAGH and the Duke of WELLINGTON; on dispatches of the Marquis WELLESLEY, and on a charge of the Bishop of WINCHESTER. The Author, when he first put forth this book, threw it down as a challenge to all the Reviewers, all the Colleges, and all the Universities. He was well aware whom he had to contend with. He was well aware of the infinite pains that would be taken to shut the door of *Schools* against his book; but it is curious enough; that, while the schoolmasters themselves have, in most cases, been afraid to put it into the hands of their scholars, lest they should incur the displeasure of the rich and the powerful, those masters do not scruple to use it for the *teaching of themselves*, in which respect, they certainly act very wisely. The day will come, when this Grammar will be in use throughout the kingdom, to the exclusion of all others; and, in the meanwhile, it is a book of greater sale than that of any one in England, to *push* the sale of which, no one single exertion has ever been made.—Price *Three Shillings*.

6. COTTAGE ECONOMY.—This little work was first published in Numbers. Its object is to inculcate *industry*, *sobriety*, and all the virtues of domestic life, amongst the labouring classes. To teach them to rely upon their own exertions, for their well being; to instil into their minds the great truth, that their happiness must mainly depend upon their own conduct; to induce them to reject the visionary notion that any benefit can arise from mere prayers and supplications without a due exertion of those faculties, which God has given them; to convince them that labour and frugality are necessary to their state of life; and that their state of life may be made the happiest state, if they have a competence therein; to teach them that a sufficiency of good food and good raiment is absolutely necessary to their

happiness, and to show them how those necessary things are to be secured. This little work, therefore, treats of the brewing of Beer, the making of Bread, the keeping of Cows, Pigs, Bees, Ewes, Goats, Poultry and Rabbits. It contains remarks relative to other matters; and the Author is well assured that in proportion that it is extensively read, the labourers of this country will be virtuous and happy. He has the pleasure to state that about thirty thousand copies of this work have been printed and sold. It has been one of the great objects of his life to make the labourers of England *well off*; and this is one of his means of furthering this great object.—Price *Two Shillings & Sixpence*.—N.B. Those who took part of the work in Numbers, may have any odd Numbers that they may want to complete their sets.

7. TREATISE ON GARDENING. This work professes in the title, to relate to Gardening in America. It was written in England the year before last, in order to fulfil a promise made to his neighbours on Long Island; but, with the difference of climate only, it is equally applicable to both countries. All the *principles* are the same; and this is a book of principles. It is useful, also, as a book which shows, in the most striking point of view, the difference in the climate of the two countries. However, its great merit is, the inculcation of sound principles with regard to *sowing, planting* and *cultivation*. The Chapter, on the preparation of land (under the head of *Soil*), should be consulted by every one, who has land to prepare for planting, with trees especially.—On the cultivation of vines, the Author thinks that all Gardeners ought to read his book. Price *Five Shillings*.

8. YEAR'S RESIDENCE IN AMERICA. This work was written at the end of the first year of the Author's residence in Long Island. The present is the *third edition*. It contains a *journal* of the weather for that year; and it contains a journal kept by an intelligent person, who went to visit the settlement of Mr. BIRKBECK. It contains a description of the Agriculture, the Roads, the Manors, the Government, the Laws and Customs of the country. The Author published the work there, as well as here. He gives an account of his own experiments in the cultivation of the Swedish Turnip, which he there cultivated by transplantation under that burning sun, and the *field*-cultivation of which useful plant he was the first to introduce into that country. He, therein, performed a service to that country, greater, he is satisfied, than ever was performed in its service, by any other foreigner; and he reflects with pleasure that he was able to render such a service to those who made his life so happy, while it was necessary for him to flee from the dungeons of Sidmouth. This book contains all information necessary for those who are about to emigrate to America. It lays all the disadvantages, as well as the advantages before them. It tells them no romantic tale; but brings them fairly acquainted with the people and with the country.—Price *Five Shillings*.

9. COBBETT'S SERMONS.—The subjects are, 1. Hypocrisy and Cruelty; 2. Drunkenness; 3. Bribery; 4. Oppression; 5. Unjust Judges; 6. The Sluggard; 7. The Murderer; 8. The Gamester; 9. Public Robbery; 10. The Unnatural Mother; 11. The Sin of Forbidding Marriage; 12. On the Duties of Parsons, and on the Institution and object of Tithes.—These Sermons were published separately, while selling in Numbers, some of them exceeded others in point of sale; but upon the whole, considering them as independent publications, upwards of a *hundred and fifty thousand* of these Sermons have

been sold; and the Author is satisfied that they have already done more real good than all the Sermons that have been published or preached in England for the last hundred years. He is well aware of the mass of prejudice which a proud and frightened Aristocracy; an interested and still more frightened body of another description; an innumerable band living upon the labour of the people unjustly; and a corrupt time-serving, envious, lying and malignant Press: he is well aware of the mass of prejudice which all these combined have been able to excite against him; but he, at the same time, knows, that in numerous instances these Sermons have been put into the hands of their own Sons and Daughters by men who detest the Author on account of his abhorrence of the political system, which causes them to fatten and the people to perish.—The whole collection forms a neat volume.—Price *Three Shillings and Sixpence.*

10. TULL'S FAMOUS WORK on the HORSE-HOEING HUS-BANDRY.—This work, which was in an old fashioned folio Volume, Mr. COBBETT has republished, in a close printed octavo volume. From this work he learned all his knowledge of the principles of Agriculture. All the numerous volumes on this science, which he had read before he read this work, he found to be of no value. He was anxious, therefore, to enable others to dip at the same fountain, at which he had dipped himself, and which had been to him the cause of so much delight. TULL was the father of the *Drill Husbandry,* not only in England, but in the world. His book is a book of real knowledge. The style, itself, is a thing infinitely useful for young people, in this day of affected expression and false ornament in writing; but the *philosophy* of the work is inestimably valuable.—There is a short introduction by Mr. COBBETT, containing an account of experiments of his own, and of others, founded on Tull's principles. The work is extremely interesting, as containing the History of the discovery of the Drill Husbandry.—Price *Thirteen Shillings and Sixpence.*

11. AMERICAN SLAVE TRADE; or, an Account of the Manner in which the Slave Dealers take Free People from some of the United States of America, and carry them away, and sell them as Slaves in other of the States; and of the horrible Cruelties practised in the carrying on of this most infamous traffic: with Reflections on the Project for forming a Colony of American Blacks in Africa, and certain Documents respecting that Project. By JESSE TORREY, Jun. Physician. With Five Plates. To which are added Notes, and a Preface, by WILLIAM COBBETT.—Price *Two Shillings,* in boards.

N.B. These works are to be had of J. M. COBBETT, No. 183, Fleet-street, London; and also, of any of the Booksellers in Paternoster-row, or of their correspondents in different parts of the Kingdom.